Praise for Conduct Gospel-Centered Funerals

Conduct Gospel-Centered Funerals is packed with wise and sane advice, ranging from how to relate to the funeral director to how to counsel a grieving family. Most importantly, the authors remind us that the gospel must be front and center at funerals. But they do not only instruct us to proclaim the gospel; they also illustrate it by including funeral sermons. This is a must-read for busy pastors, and I suspect most pastors will turn to it often.

Thomas R. Schreiner, James Buchanan Harrison
professor of New Testament interpretation at
The Southern Baptist Theological Seminary

I needed this book thirty-five years ago! In an age where funerals and weddings are likely to be the only occasions when the gospel is heard, the need to view a funeral service as an occasion for the *evangel* is paramount. Every gospel-centered minister needs to read this book.

Derek W. H. Thomas, John E. Richards professor of systematic
and practical theology at Reformed Theological Seminary

Conduct Gospel-Centered Funerals is wonderfully practical and helpful. The authors have performed hundreds of God-honoring funerals and here share lessons learned in the trenches. If you are called on to perform funerals, you will find this resource invaluable. I know I will consult it often.

Mike McKinley, senior pastor at Sterling Park Baptist Church,
Sterling, Virginia, and author of Church Planting Is for Wimps

Funerals are one of the greatest opportunities for the gospel of Jesus Christ to be proclaimed because they are reminders to everyone that death is indeed "the end of all men." Brian Croft and Phil Newton know the gospel well, and in this book they share their seasoned pastoral wisdom.

Tom Ascol, pastor of Grace Baptist Church, Cape Coral,
Florida, and executive director of Founders Ministries

This theologically grounded guide is commendable for the way it leads readers to understand the central role that the gospel should have in funeral sermons, eulogies, and musical selections. It is worthy of careful and reflective reading by pastors, church leaders, and ministerial students.

David S. Dockery, president of Union University

Brian Croft and Phil Newton are faithful, reliable guides helping the pastor with everything from prefuneral planning to postfuneral pastoral care. Particularly helpful is chapter 3, which guides the pastor in crafting gospel-centered messages for various types of funerals. In short, this is the first book pastors should consult for planning and preaching funerals.

Bruce Ashford, dean of The College at Southeastern and associate professor of philosophy and intercultural studies at Southeastern Baptist Theological Seminary

This is an outstanding book that I wish had been available decades ago! Every pastor, elder, and man preparing for the ministry should read and apply its counsel.

Paul Tautges, pastor-teacher at Immanuel Bible Church, Sheboygan, Wisconsin, and author of Comfort Those Who Grieve

Not everything in *Conduct Gospel-Centered Funerals* will fit every pastoral situation or cultural context, but every pastor will find much-needed guidance on what to say and do as they tread carefully and prayerfully through the minefields of bereavement, mourning, and funeral arrangements.

David Murray, professor of Old Testament and practical theology at Puritan Reformed Theological Seminary

Brian Croft and Phil Newton write out of a passion for Christ and a yearning to see the lost saved and believers edified in the conduct of gospel-based funerals. New pastors will especially benefit from their practical insights in planning, preparing, preaching, and practicing funerals. And veteran pastors will be challenged to make sure mourners are comforted with the pure word of God, with a clear vision of Christ in the words and actions of the pastor.

Andrew Davis, senior pastor at First Baptist Church, Durham, North Carolina

CONDUCT GOSPEL-CENTERED FUNERALS

Other Books in the Practical Shepherding Series

Prepare Them to Shepherd

Visit the Sick

CONDUCT GOSPEL-CENTERED FUNERALS

REVISED AND UPDATED

Applying the Gospel at the Unique Challenges of Death

BRIAN CROFT
AND PHIL A. NEWTON

ZONDERVAN

Conduct Gospel-Centered Funerals
Copyright © 2014 by Brian Croft and Phil Newton

Previously published in 2011 by Day One Publications under the same title.

This title is also available as a Zondervan ebook.
Visit www.zondervan.com/ebooks.

Requests for information should be addressed to:

Zondervan, 3900 *Sparks Dr. SE, Grand Rapids, Michigan 49546*

Library of Congress Cataloging-in-Publication Data

Croft, Brian.
    Conduct gospel-centered funerals : applying the gospel at the
unique challenges of death / Brian Croft and Phil A. Newton.
        p. cm.– (Practical shepherding series)
        ISBN 978-0-310-51718-4 (softcover)
        1. Funeral service. I. Newton, Phil A. II. Title.
    BV199.F8C76 2014
    265'.85–dc23   2013041223

Cover design and illustrations: Jay Smith-Juicebox Designs
Interior design: Matthew Van Zomeren

Printed in the United States of America

HB 07.10.2024

To our fathers,
Bill Croft and Joe E. Newton

CONTENTS

Foreword by Daniel Akin 11

INTRODUCTION 13

Chapter 1
PLAN *(PHIL NEWTON)*. 17

Chapter 2
PREPARE *(BRIAN CROFT)* 39

Chapter 3
PREACH *(PHIL NEWTON)* 53

Chapter 4
PERFORM *(BRIAN CROFT)* 72

Acknowledgments 81
*Appendix 1: Examples of Funeral Sermons
    (Phil Newton)* 85
*Appendix 2: Examples of Fitting Eulogies
    (Brian Croft)*. 107
*Appendix 3: Examples of Appropriate Music
    (Phil Newton with Jim Carnes)* 119
*Appendix 4: Examples of Order of Funeral Services
    (Brian Croft)*. 123
Notes 125

FOREWORD

SOMETIMES BIG THINGS come in small packages. This book is, without question, one of those occasions. Ministers have two unique opportunities to share the gospel—when there is a wedding, and when there is a funeral. The former is almost always a happy gathering of family and friends. The latter, on the other hand, is one of mixed emotions and feelings. Sorrow, of course, is always present. The gospel has its proper place at both, but it is especially needed when we are confronted with death and our mortality. People need to hear that there is hope in Christ, that death is not the end, that sin does not have the final word. With wisdom and careful preparation, the faithful minister must point those who are before him to the salvation that is found only in Jesus Christ. He must take them to a bloody cross and an empty tomb. He must preach the good news of the gospel.

How this can be done well is the goal of this book, and Brian Croft and Phil Newton have met that challenge. This short work is pastorally rich, theologically faithful, and practically useful. It is a book that should be used in Bible colleges and seminaries, and it should be on the shelf of every minister who, as John Baxter said, preaches as a dying man to dying men. Brian and Phil show us how we can minister to the hurting as we point them to the victory we have in Christ. During times of grief and sorrow people need to hear from God. They need to hear the gospel.

Conduct Gospel-Centered Funerals

Funerals provide a rare opportunity to speak truth into the lives of many who never read the Bible, seldom-if-ever attend church, and avoid spiritual issues when possible. We must not miss the opportunity we have been given as pastors and evangelists. This book is a marvelous gift to the body of Christ that will help us to faithfully honor both callings. I hope it will be widely distributed. I am glad to give it my strongest possible commendation.

Daniel L. Akin, president of Southeastern Baptist Theological Seminary, Wake Forest, North Carolina

INTRODUCTION

WHAT DOES IT MEAN to be gospel-centered? We hear this term almost incessantly today, but we should never presume everyone knows what it means. Here is my attempt at a definition: *Gospel-centeredness is making sure the foundation of our hope is rooted in a holy God's merciful plan to redeem sinners by crushing his own Son on the cross in our place, and proclaiming Christ's triumph over death in his resurrection and the future promise of our own resurrection when Christ returns.*

It is especially important to be gospel-centered in the context of a funeral. Many pastors think they are being faithful to the gospel of Jesus Christ, when in actuality they are not. That is why we have written this short volume. There is a pressing need, not just for a book on the practical matters related to leading a funeral service, but also for a guide that offers a clear understanding of what the gospel is and its appropriate application in the context of death. Sadly, it is all too easy to confuse the clear gospel message—even in the midst of a funeral.

The gospel is frequently obscured when a pastor offers comfort about heaven when *how* heaven is received is not made clear. The gospel is distorted when a pastor preaches the deceased into eternal glory with no credible evidence of gospel transformation in that person's life. The gospel is contradicted when the man entrusted to facilitate and conduct the funeral service is unloving, impatient, and uninterested in the souls of the family members who remain. As pastors, both of us share a burden to see the gospel clearly and winsomely proclaimed when funerals are held. We have attended too many funerals at which the gospel was never mentioned or, if it was, was not presented as the focus and source of our hope in Christ. The gospel of Jesus Christ was lamentably overlooked as the primary purpose of the service—where our true hope should rest.

Gospel-centeredness is making the gospel of Jesus Christ the primary purpose *and* focus of the funeral. We plan, prepare, preach, and perform gospel-centered funerals in the same way we would pursue Christ and our hope of salvation in him as the central focus in our gatherings, our homes, our marriages, and all the other areas of our lives. Funerals pose unique situations and challenges that can leave a pastor unsure how to magnify Christ in the fog of the details and demands.

The aim of this book is to do more than inform you. Yes, we will cover the logistics, challenges, and practical matters of leading a funeral. But we want to also show you how to apply the power of the gospel in the midst of these unique challenges. So, for example, if the funeral you are conducting is for a young man tragically killed—extend the hope of Christ to his friends and family. Even though a baby has died—exhort the parents to look to Christ. Even though the family of the deceased is fighting among themselves and the funeral director has been less than helpful to work with—point them to Christ as you conduct yourself in a way that reflects him. As ministers of the gospel of Jesus Christ, our chief aim (as we argue in the pages of this book) is to bring God glory by making much of Jesus in all circumstances and situations—especially funerals.

Introduction

Consider our experiences. Learn from our mistakes. Renew a deep love for our Savior. Most of all, be encouraged that the clear message of the gospel of Jesus Christ can and should be ministered at every funeral. Be faithful by clearly presenting the hope that Jesus offers us in his death and resurrection.

CHAPTER 1

PLAN

Phil Newton

> When he hears of afflictions of any kind coming upon households, he [the minister] should not wait to be sent for, but should hasten to them with the rich consolations he gathers from the gospel.
>
> Thomas Murphy, *Pastoral Theology: The Pastor in the Various Duties of His Office*

FUNERALS TEND TO ARRIVE at a minister's doorstep with little advance notice. Though you can sometimes anticipate a funeral in the case of an extended illness, most come rather suddenly and unexpectedly. An accident, a heart attack, an aggressive illness, a rapidly growing cancer, an undetected disease, a birth defect, a suicide—all of these tend to come without warning. As a minister of the gospel, you must be prepared.

In This Chapter

- Understanding the minister's role during deaths...
- Recognizing dos and don'ts of funeral arrangements...
- Preparing to work with the local funeral home...

Conduct Gospel-Centered Funerals

Your Pastoral Care Responsibility

The responsibility for the pastoral care of the family belongs to you. There are six areas of responsibility you need to consider.

Offering Guidance and Care

The death of a family member is a significant event, one for which your church members will need shepherding and guidance. It is a time to apply the gospel and its promises to help a grieving family through the rough, churning waters they must navigate. One of our church families went through the trial of watching their newborn struggle with an undetected birth defect during his first month. They spent over three months in the local children's hospital, with either the mom or dad constantly by the child's side. I visited with them frequently, always reading Scripture, talking of God's promises, reflecting on the gospel, and praying for them and their little boy. We shed many tears during that time, and my wife and I were there with them when he breathed his last breath. We were comforted by the sufficiency of the gospel at that time. Later, when I conducted the two memorial services for this little boy (one with our church, the other in the dad's hometown several hours away), I was able to *build* on the pastoral conversations I'd had with the family. We all gloried in the gospel of Christ, and despite the intense sadness felt at the loss, we found comfort in the work of Jesus Christ.

Offering Comfort through the Word and Your Presence

Bring comfort both through the Scriptures and by your physical presence. Just being present means much to a grieving family. Sometimes a minister thinks he needs to come up with some pithy quote or wise saying to help a grieving family. Better instead is the minister's comforting presence as one who loves and cares for the family. Listen to them, offer a consoling arm around the shoulders, read from God's word, and pray with them. All of this means much more than a clever phrase. They are unlikely to remember much of what you say, but they will remember that you stood with them in their loss. What is most likely to stick with them are the particular biblical texts you select to share, with some members of the grieving family recalling the passages years later. I recently had this experience as one of our older members reminded me of a particular text that I had read to her during a period of grief many years ago. I had completely forgotten about it, but that memory has remained with her over the years.

Representing Christ, the Church, and the Gospel

As a minister of the gospel, you represent Jesus Christ, the church, and the gospel you proclaim. The minister visibly represents Christ's ministry to the family. It's not your job to replace Christ—that could never happen! But you are called to come alongside as one who has been in the presence of Christ through the word and prayer, and to now stand with this grieving family. Pastors are often the first face of the church to be present in grief and the first to apply the gospel to their circumstances to help them move forward in hope and faith. Ministers should also be alert to ways in which other members of the church can aid a family in distress, helping the body to provide care for its members in need.

As one who represents the gospel, a minister should never settle for simply telling the family what he thinks they want to hear. First and foremost, a minister of the gospel must be faithful to the gospel of Jesus Christ. I once attended a funeral of a man who had been very active until late-term cancer struck him down. Until just a few months prior to his death, this man appeared quite youthful—even though he was in his seventies. One of the pastors at the funeral, instead of being straightforward about the promises of the gospel, twisted a well-known gospel passage in a way that accommodated what he believed would please the family and the man's friends. He quoted John 3:3 ("no one can see the kingdom of God unless they are born again") and told the story of Nicodemus's visit with Jesus. Yet rather than talking about the new birth, he said to them, "You see, Nicodemus wanted to remain youthful. He went to Jesus because he wanted to keep on living a full, youthful life." A sermon about the need to be born again was twisted into an approval of the pursuit of a youthful, athletic lifestyle. This pastor commended the deceased as one who shared the spirit embodied in Nicodemus, approving of his desire for youthful vigor. Needless to say, I was grieved that this man had twisted and demeaned the gospel rather than applying it for the comfort of the family.

Declaring the Sufficiency of the Gospel

A minister should be "all about" the gospel. By this, I do not mean that you should exploit the grieving process for the sole purpose of evangelism. Evangelism *might* present itself during this time of pastoral care, but the minister's primary goal is to help the family understand that the gospel is about living *and* dying. The same gospel that gives us joy in life also gives us joy when facing death. As the incarnate Son, Jesus Christ triumphed over death, freeing those who trust him from slavery to the fear of death (Hebrews 2:14 – 15). The minister's task is to help the family live in this truth.

But what do you do if the deceased family member was not a believer? How can you, as a minister, offer hope to the family? First, you need to be careful to avoid "preaching a person into heaven." If the deceased offered no fruit or evidence of conversion, you should be cautious and not assume he or she was a believer. At the same time, you must learn to walk the tightrope of not passing judgment on one's eternal state. If the deceased had professed to be a Christian but showed little evidence of this, you can refer to the person's profession but carefully avoid confidently declaring that this person has passed into heaven. I have done numerous funerals where there was scant evidence of genuine faith. Yet we need to realize that ultimately this is not our call to make. So I might say, "Mr. Brown professed Jesus Christ as his Savior as a young man" and then avoid mentioning this again. Or I might choose to share a conversation I had with a spouse or relative about this: "Sally told me of a time, years ago, when Mr. Brown professed faith in Christ; we rejoice in this report." In other words, *do not say more than what you are assured of by the deceased person's walk with Christ.* If the deceased scandalized the gospel by his or her life — despite an earlier profession — it may be best to avoid referring to their supposed profession at all, lest those listening become confused about the demands of the gospel.

In a similar way, you will also want to refrain from preaching the deceased into eternal perdition! I remember an occasion when I was working for my dad at a funeral when the minister used very clear language to declare that the deceased was now under eternal judgment.* He lightly cloaked it in judgment terminology, but it was clear enough to all of us what he was saying. And he was probably right, though I question the prudence of making an announcement like this at that time. Most of those in attendance were not under any pretense that this man had been welcomed in the presence of Christ. Rather, he could have more judiciously said, "It is only those who have trusted in Jesus Christ and his redemptive work who will be forever in his presence," or something along those lines. Place the emphasis not on the deceased but rather on appeals to the living, urging them to trust in Christ.

Building Deeper Relationships

The occasion of death is a wonderful opportunity for developing deep relationships through ministry to the immediate and extended family. Walking with members of my congregation in their grief has put me into closer relationship with them. They rarely put on a front at such times. Their pain comes to the surface in comments that might otherwise never be uttered. As a minister, you will see people as they are, raw and unfiltered. You may hear things that surprise you; you may see attitudes surface that you had never noticed before. Build on these moments. The grieving period itself is not the best time to attack those areas of needed sanctification that surface in a church member's life. But as time passes, in the forthcoming weeks and months, a watchful minister will find that he is able to apply the teaching of Scripture to issues he recognizes

---

* My dad worked as a funeral director.

in a grieving family. You may be able to recommend books to read that steer a person toward further spiritual development. Or you might want to pair the grieving person with someone else in the church who will come alongside as an encourager in the faith.

Being Ready to Offer Long-Term Counsel
The conclusion of a funeral service does not mean the end of your care for the family. A family's grief may be tender for weeks, months, and even years after the death of a family member or loved one. Offering a word in season, a visit, a phone call, an e-mail, or a note will be welcomed and appreciated long after the funeral is over. Offer an acknowledgment on the anniversary marking the loved one's death and your thoughtfulness and care will certainly be appreciated.

Making and Carrying Out Funeral Arrangements
There are many details to stay on top of in planning a funeral. As a minister, you also want to be aware of appropriate actions that will best serve the grieving family. What follows is a list of appropriate dos and don'ts to offer you some direction.

The Dos
1. DO try to be with the family as soon as you receive word about the family member's death. Your warm presence and tender words may be just what the family needs. Your first visit need not be long. Many people prefer privacy as they grieve, so be sensitive to this. Plan on maintaining contact with the family by means of phone calls and visits. Take along another elder or deacon who would be sensitive to the grieving, so they

can add their comfort and so you can train them in caring for the grieving.

2. DO offer to help the family gather information in preparation for the funeral arrangements. Offer to assist in enlisting pallbearers and making calls as needed on behalf of the family. Discuss where the internment will take place and make plans for music for the funeral service.

3. DO mobilize the church family to join you in caring for the needs of the family. Offer to arrange for people who can provide food, house out-of-town relatives, or assist in readying the house for guests and provide child care for little ones. Bible study and small group leaders will likely want to join you in caring for the family members. Make appropriate phone calls to ensure that leaders are mobilized.

4. DO gently offer suggestions that might make the funeral service more honoring to Christ. A minister might say, "I know you have much on your mind as you make plans for the memorial service. If your family is agreeable, may I suggest that we sing congregationally and read some gospel-centered Scripture during the service? If we can aim to have an abbreviated worship service, I think you will find great comfort in thinking about Jesus Christ and his promises." Sometimes musical selections can detract from the good news of Jesus Christ. A minister may not be able to persuade the family otherwise, but you should at least attempt to offer good suggestions on music and Scripture. Engaging the congregation in singing helps to promote the gospel — if appropriate hymns are selected.*

---

* See appendix 3 for a list of suggested hymn selections.

I once conducted a funeral for an elderly lady who had been a lifelong Catholic. Her daughter and son-in-law had been radically converted to Christ and had become members of our church. We discussed the service, and I suggested we sing a couple of hymns. We knew the attendance at the funeral would be sparse, but we also knew there would be a number of unbelievers present. So we intentionally chose gospel-rich hymns that our church members knew well. (Yes, I realize many unbelievers are unaccustomed to singing in a church, but why not give them the opportunity?) Afterward, having heard the songs and the preaching of the gospel, one of the deceased lady's longtime friends told her daughter (a faithful believer) that she needed to talk with her. She shared, "I think I believe what I heard today."

5. *DO be personal without forgetting that your primary responsibility is to set forth the gospel of Jesus Christ.* Anecdotes about the deceased are certainly appropriate, although they should be shared wisely. For the funeral of a believer, the goal is that attendees will leave thinking, "What a great Savior this person had!" rather than what a clever fellow or gifted woman they were. Anecdotes may be drawn from your own relationship with the deceased or uncovered through conversations you have with their family or friends. Use caution here and try to avoid discussing private issues or matters that might lead to embarrassment or a breach of confidentiality. Also, be careful not to tell a story in order to manipulate people into a particular emotional response. Your task is to bring comfort, not to manipulate. A light or humorous story or illustration may be appropriate, but act wisely. I once attended a funeral where it

was just one story after another about the deceased. None of them related to Christ. Not even the minister spoke of Christ, other than a token nod to him in his prayer. Most of the service focused on sharing humorous incidents or idiosyncrasies of the deceased. I left thinking that while the stories were interesting, no comfort had been offered and an opportunity for speaking of the hope in the gospel of Christ had been squandered.

In contrast to this experience, I recall attending the funeral of an older woman who had been an educator and coach in her community. One of the family members told of how the woman had come to faith in Christ after her teenage daughter suggested she read Chuck Colson's *Born Again*. While numerous delightful anecdotes were told about this lively person, the centerpiece of the funeral was a clear gospel message given by her son-in-law. The church was packed with people from the community, and they left without a doubt that Jesus Christ and the gospel were the focus of this beloved woman's life.

6. DO expound the Scriptures. Many pastors have a habit of stringing together a series of Scripture passages for a funeral service. But any sense of context is missing in this approach. Scripture should always be understood in context, not pulled and mashed into something new. I knew of an older minister who had committed much of Scripture to memory, and his funeral messages consisted of quoting dozens and dozens of verses. While I believe strongly in the primacy of the God's word, try to be sensitive to the way in which you use a biblical passage. Some preachers, with the best intentions, lead hearers to misconstrue the meaning of a passage. As a college student attending a funeral, I heard a minister use 1 Corinthians 2:9

from the NASB as his text: "But just as it is written, 'Things which eye has not seen and ear has not heard, and which have not entered the heart of man, all that God has prepared for those who love Him.'" He went on to speak of how wonderful a place heaven would be for the deceased. If he had read the next verse, though, he would have seen that this text has nothing to do with heaven—it speaks of the believer's present provisions through Christ in the gospel!

Instead of choosing an assortment of texts, select a single text or two and open it up by explaining it to the congregation and making application in light of the gospel. There are several "standard" funeral texts such as Psalm 23; Psalm 27; Psalm 46; Ecclesiastes 3:1–11; John 11:1–44; John 14:1–7; 1 Corinthians 15; 1 Thessalonians 4:13–18; and Revelation 21–22. In truth, almost any passage from the Gospels or a passage that explains the gospel of Christ will work well. I once preached on justification by faith from Romans 3 at one family's request. It ended up being a clear gospel explanation and gave further opportunity for gospel discussions after the service. At another funeral, I focused on the person and work of Christ from Colossians 1:15–20 to an audience that, for the most part, had a law-based, works-righteousness understanding of salvation. It was a priceless opportunity to make the gospel of Christ clear to them. At my dad's funeral, I expounded Revelation 5, making appropriate gospel exhortations throughout. I personally profited from a meditation on resting in Jesus from Matthew 11:28–30 at the funeral service for my granddaughter.

7. DO dress appropriately. Though a black suit is not necessary, a dark suit with a white or blue shirt and a conservative tie is often appropriate. Customs in your region may dictate otherwise, but normally this will keep you appropriately dressed. If you are new to an area, you might want to ask the local funeral director what to wear. He or she will be in a good position to advise you. Don't forget to take an overcoat with you for winter graveside services, especially in cold-weather parts of the country. The coldest I have ever been in my life was while conducting a winter graveside service. The burial was on the crest of a hill in the cemetery, and I shivered throughout, making speaking quite difficult! Shortly after the service, I found myself a better overcoat!

8. *DO get the details about the graveside service.* If there is an internment service or graveside service, the minister will usually need to wait by the rear door of the funeral coach and arrive with the procession. He will lead the pallbearers with the casket to the grave site. This might seem like a strange warning, but exercise caution as you are walking near the grave site. I've found that grave digging does not always go as planned, and the width of the grave can present a slight danger for a fall. Those who prepare the grave usually place boards along the edge of the grave to prevent accidents, and these boards are covered with "funeral grass" (an Astroturf-type material), so you may not see them. Either walk around the boards or directly on them if you are instructed to do so by the director or cemetery attendant. Believe it or not, I have seen pallbearers unwittingly step into a grave!

You will need to stand at the head of the casket to offer your remarks at the graveside. Begin your remarks only after the director gives you a nod to proceed. I always keep my eye on the director, as he watches to make sure that all those in the procession have arrived. Once he catches your eye and signals, you can begin your remarks. Do not count on having a lectern or stand to assist with your Bible and notes. Normally, these are *not* provided in the cemetery. I recommend clipping your notes to the pages of your Bible or placing them in a small notebook or three-ring binder that you can use at the funeral.

After you finish your remarks and end with prayer, you may need to quietly speak to family members seated by the graveside. A brief but warm comment, a handshake, or a hug is appropriate. After you speak with family members, the funeral director will close the graveside service, giving instructions to the guests.

9. DO offer your services to the funeral home when they do not have a minister to serve a grieving family. Gospel opportunities await those who minister on these occasions. You will be frequently introduced to people who need to see Christianity at work and hear of God's good news for sinners. You may want to invite members from your congregation to assist in serving these families in need.

The Don'ts

1. DON'T try to do the funeral directors' job. Remember that they are professionals. Instead, consult with them to find out the logistics of where you need to be prior to the service, where you need to sit, and how you will close the service and turn the reins back to the director. Avoid telling a funeral director how to do his or her job.

2. DON'T squander an opportunity to counsel with the gospel of Christ. Funerals are a chance to apply what you preach and teach your congregation. Often, you will find that passages you've recently preached will be useful in your ministry as you point the attendees' attention back to some particular application of the Scripture you made earlier.

3. DON'T be late for the funeral. Arrive early to spend time with the family and guests. Let the parking lot attendant (if one is available) know that you are the minister for the funeral. He may ask you to park in a special place at the head of the funeral procession. The funeral director will normally be awaiting your arrival with a "minister's card" (or "obituary card," as it may be called) that gives you basic information on the deceased's birth, hometown, family, etc. You may want to use some of this information in the service, even if only as a guide to praying for the family members by name. Once you arrive, introduce yourself to the director, ask about logistics with the family and any plans for the procession, and give him or her an order for the funeral service—particularly specifying how you will close the service and return leadership to the director. Find out the details for the graveside or internment service. He may invite you to ride in the director's car. I always prefer doing so. You will get to know the director, plus you are guaranteed to arrive at the appropriate place for the burial! To be honest, whenever I am asked to be the lead car I have a fear I will end up leading the procession to the wrong spot in the cemetery, so it may be best to stick with the director, if they offer.

4. DON'T neglect communicating with those involved in the memorial service. If other members of your congregation are participating in some aspect of the service, make sure you are all on the same page. I had an unfortunate experience in a church I previously served when a woman with a wonderful singing voice had been asked to sing at the funeral for a relative of another church member. The service was held in a rural location some thirty to forty minutes from our church, and it was not easy to find! This woman was notorious for being late, and sure enough, when it came time for us to process into the church to begin the service, the singer was nowhere to be found. Charitably, the director delayed the start in hope that the woman would soon arrive. After an uncomfortable delay in the afternoon sun, she remained a no-show. We began the service, and ten minutes later the singer sheepishly made her way to a seat close to the front. In what goes down as one of my most awkward funeral moments, I closed the service, walked in front of the casket, and began to exit toward the adjacent cemetery. Having gone no more than twenty feet, the deceased's widow blurted out, "Let the girl sing!" The director glanced at me, motioned with his eyes to return, and moved the casket once again to the front of the little church so that "the girl" could sing. A little margin in timing and better communication on my part might have alleviated that tense moment.

5. *DON'T preach too long at the funeral service.* On Sunday mornings, I regularly preach forty-five to fifty minute sermons. At funerals, I only speak for ten to twenty minutes. There have been a few rare exceptions, but only at the family's request. Why do I keep my messages short? It is very difficult for people to maintain a long attention span during a funeral. Brevity also shows consideration for those who have taken time off from work to attend the service and who need to return

after it is over. A typical funeral service should normally last no more than thirty to forty minutes. Even a brief service can accomplish much good for the kingdom of God in that time frame. There are exceptions, of course. I've attended services that lasted well over an hour and were done appropriately. I've also attended services that lasted that long and were done inappropriately, straining everyone in attendance. Family members may be emotionally exhausted, so your aim is to offer them comfort, *not* add to their exhaustion.

6. DON'T do more than you are asked to do. Sometimes multiple ministers will be invited to fill various roles in a service. One might be asked to read Scripture, another to offer the eulogy, and another to give the sermon. Do only what you've been asked to do. Assuming that you have liberty to go beyond the family's wishes betrays the confidence they have placed in you. I was asked to read a biblical text at a funeral without offering any commentary on the text. I feared that the minister would fail to preach the gospel, so I really wanted to say more! Even though my fears were realized, I restrained my impulse to speak. Trusting in the power of God's word, I prayed that the Spirit would powerfully attend the reading of Holy Scripture. Out of respect for the family, I dared not take advantage of my time on the platform by misusing my opportunity.

Gathering Information

Sitting with a family just after their loved one has died provides a precious opportunity to understand their affection (or, in some cases, lack of affection) for the deceased. You can invite them to tell stories and to remember the little things that the deceased had done for them or with them. Sharing these types of stories will give a unique perspective of the deceased, as you begin to see them more like the family does. I've found it appropriate, especially after the initial shock of the loved one's death, to ask questions that allow the family to open up and talk. It is certainly appropriate to jot down notes in the family's presence as you prepare for the service. You do not want to misrepresent a story they share, so pay close attention to details, asking questions to clarify anything you don't understand.

Working with the Funeral Home

You are not alone in caring for families when a death occurs. The local funeral home will also be involved, albeit from a different perspective. My father was a funeral director during my childhood and adolescence, and I had the opportunity to watch him as he cared for people. I noticed his concern as families made their way through the shock of death and the subsequent grieving process. Though he rarely talked about it, his care was evident in his actions and his tenderness that often went far beyond normal funeral "service" to help people through their grief.

My father was certainly not the only one who cared like this. Through the years, I've met many funeral directors and personnel who compassionately serve those who experienced the loss of a family member. For some it is just a job, but honestly, it is difficult to work in an environment in which you regularly face death and grief unless there is at least some small measure of concern for the grieving. As a gospel minister, I encourage you to seek out funeral home personnel who will partner with you in offering genuine care for people.

Conduct Gospel-Centered Funerals

Knowing the Funeral Director

In the small town of my early years, there were two funeral homes and two funeral directors, with a few employees between them. Local ministers had little trouble knowing the name of the directors and having some congenial relationship with them. That is still true in smaller communities. But since most people now live in urban areas, it is difficult to personally know the funeral director. In some cases, large conglomerates own funeral homes rather than a local family. Multiple funeral homes will conduct several funerals each day instead of the four or five per week typical in a small community. Naturally, the director has less leisure time to spend chatting with local ministers, so a minister may have to take the initiative and introduce himself to the funeral directors at the local funeral homes. Here are a few suggestions for your visit:

1. Make an appointment to visit for five to ten minutes with the funeral directors in your area.
2. Leave him or her a business card and a little information about yourself and your church.
3. Ask about the funeral home's policies for meeting with families, funeral services, and funerals for those who don't have burial insurance.
4. Ask for a quick tour of the facilities so you will be familiar with what services are available for members of your congregation.
5. Keep a record of the director's name, phone number, and any details that might help you to be an informed counselor to those involved in loss.

Plan

Understanding Logistics

What is the funeral director's role? We've spent some time considering the role of the minister when someone dies, but we haven't talked much about the other member of the team who cares for the grieving family — the funeral director. They have an important job to do as well, and as I mentioned earlier, it's vital that the minister not attempt to take over the funeral director's domain. I remember my dad commenting, with much displeasure, about two pastors in our county who always tried to take over his job. My dad was an experienced professional at his work and well respected by his peers. The pastors in question were not experienced at funerals, but they liked to be in charge — even pastors are not immune to pride. I still recall my father expressing his dread whenever he had to team up with these two pastors to do funerals. They were a poor witness to my father and to his other employees. These pastors should have understood what the funeral director was charged with doing in behalf of the family. To help you avoid repeating their mistakes, we'll consider some of the key components of the funeral home director's job description.

Provide respectful care of the deceased family member. The funeral director is the last one to give physical care to the remains of the deceased. I remember, as I worked with my dad, the tenderness and respect he showed to the lifeless body. Although no one was around to see how he handled his work, grieving family members had confidence that "Mr. Joe" would treat their loved one with the greatest respect.

Provide short-term service for the family. Though the pastor is engaged long-term, the funeral home is involved for only a few days in the lives of grieving family members. Most funeral directors want to provide the best possible care in that brief span. What services does the funeral home typically provide?

- transport of the deceased's body for embalming and preparation
- assisting the family in making arrangements for the service
- providing a range of caskets, vaults, and clothing for the deceased
- seeking to make the lifeless face as natural as possible
- gathering and arrange floral tributes
- notifying the local newspaper of the death
- transporting the deceased and floral tributes to the place of service and internment
- arranging for details at the graveside
- making sure the grave is ready for the family's visit
- filing a death certificate

My dad often reminded me that he could not afford to make mistakes since he dealt with people for such a brief period of time. Any mistakes would be remembered and would reflect negatively on him and his work.

Accommodate the wishes of the family. The funeral director normally meets with the family within twenty-four hours of their loved one's death. He gathers needed information for legal purposes, for the minister, and for ensuring that every desire of the family is met. Occasionally, the pastor may need to accompany the family at such time, although for the most part, that visit should be left to the funeral director. The director will ask for the deceased's full name, place and date of birth, place of residence, place of death, names of family members, place of employment, church membership, other significant organizations or involvement, names of pallbearers, location of the funeral service, name of the person who will conduct the service, name of the person responsible for music, and location of the cemetery for burial. I have found, especially with younger families experiencing a death, that it is helpful to clue them in on what will happen at the visit with the director. At that time, he will also offer various selections of caskets, vaults, and burial clothing. On numerous occasions, I have been seated with a family around a table, helping them gather the information they need for their meeting with the director.

Comply with the laws of the state. Every legal jurisdiction has laws regulating burial and cremation of the deceased. The funeral director will be familiar with the current laws and responsible to fulfill them.

～

Attention to detail helps the minister to serve grieving families as well as to provide a good witness in the community. Since most deceased are buried three to five days after death, the minister will need to be well organized and prepared for what seems a rushed period. Thinking ahead for what the family will encounter in the brief time frame between death and burial will enable a minister to focus on ways to apply the gospel to families struggling with their loss.

I suggest periodically reviewing this chapter (and the ones that follow) until your understanding of how to prepare for a funeral service becomes a natural part of your ministry to the church.

CHAPTER 2

PREPARE

Brian Croft

> O then, as you expect peace or rest in the chambers of death, get union with Christ. A grave with Christ is a comfortable place.
>
> John Flavel, "Christ's Funeral Illustrated, in Its Manner, Reasons, and Excellent Ends"

PASTORS ALWAYS HAVE MUCH TO PREPARE—in any season of ministry. If we are not preaching, we are preparing to preach. If we are not leading a meeting, we are preparing to lead. Most of these activities are known ahead of time. We know when we are to preach on Sunday. We know when meetings have been planned. But funerals are different. Funerals get dropped into our schedule unannounced, and they can be challenging to prepare. There are two reasons for this.

First, there is the

In This Chapter
- Preparing for the funeral service...
- Understanding the graveside service...
- Tending to the pastor's heart...

need for a quick turnaround. Death comes when we least expect it and at some of the most inconvenient times. Typically, a pastor will have between two to five days to plan and prepare for all that comes with a funeral. It gets crammed into his schedule for the week or other previously planned meetings must be pushed back. So he will need to discern which tasks will need to wait. Because the time is short, preparation for a funeral should actually begin long before a phone call from a family is received. In truth, funeral preparation begins as the pastor is involved in faithfully shepherding the lives of his people.

Every funeral is unique in its own way because pastors immerse themselves in the life of a family that has been deeply affected and forever changed by the death. Every family has its own tensions, dysfunctions, and quirks, all of which are heightened in the beginning stages of the grieving process. This creates emotional and mental exhaustion for the family—and for the one entrusted to plan and prepare for the funeral.

The aim of this chapter is to provide a helpful template to aid in preparing, while also covering some details that relate to leading a funeral service.

The Funeral Service

Opening a funeral service can feel just as awkward as those first words you speak to a family that has just lost their loved one. Yet, because of the attentiveness of people in those moments, we must seize the opportunity to choose these words carefully, as they will set the tone for the entire service.

Prepare

A good rule of thumb is to allow God to speak before you do. Though different kinds of people attend a funeral, they are all, in their own way, asking the same question, "*Why, God?*" Choose a passage of Scripture that cuts through the questions, the sorrow, and the skepticism and declares the unchanging character of our great God. For example, you might begin by standing, moving to the pulpit, and then saying something like, "Hear these words about our great, unchanging God":

> The LORD is righteous in all his ways
>   and faithful in all he does.
> The LORD is near to all who call on him,
>   to all who call on him in truth.
> He fulfills the desires of those who fear him;
>   he hears their cry and saves them.
> The LORD watches over all who love him,
>   but all the wicked he will destroy.
> My mouth will speak in praise of the LORD.
>   Let every creature praise his holy name
>   for ever and ever.

Psalm 145:17 – 21

God's words will always be more powerful, profound, and pervasive than our own. So begin by allowing God to pierce through the doubts. Then share some words of welcome for those attending and simply state why you have gathered. The rest of the funeral service can be broadly outlined around five areas: prayer, music, Scripture readings, eulogy, and sermon. For each, make sure you are asking yourself how the gospel can be accurately presented.

Conduct Gospel-Centered Funerals

Prayer

Prayers can be staggered throughout the service, and you can involve different people. Make sure that if you allow someone else to pray in the service, you know them and have confidence they will pray in a way that is respectful of the direction you have chosen for the service. In the planning for a funeral I was asked to conduct recently, some members of the family asked if their Catholic priest could say a prayer during the service as well. I tried to graciously explain why that wouldn't be possible, assuming that the priest and I would have fairly different theological understandings and ways of praying during the service. Choose wisely the hills you want to die on as you prepare. Make sure the issues aren't of secondary importance—that they revolve around whether or not the gospel will be confused, not around your personal preferences. In this case, I would rather have the family be upset with me than risk confusing the gospel by having a Catholic priest pray for the soul of the person who had died!

What should you pray for? Make sure you pray for the spouse, the children and grandchildren, and the friends of the deceased, as well as for their other acquaintances—that they would be comforted by God, find their hope in the gospel, and grieve in a way that honors God and the person they've gathered to remember.

Music

There are a few things to consider as you prepare the music for the service. First, ask the family if they have songs they suggest for the service. Find out how music is typically done at the location where the funeral will be held. Find out what kind of equipment is available, as this will determine whether the music can be done live or must be prerecorded. Be discerning as to who you allow to sing in the service and what they will sing.

When it comes time to choose the music, do all you can to accommodate the family while still realizing there are doctrinal lines to draw in the sand and preference lines you can bend on. Select songs that will reflect the Savior and try to intersperse them throughout the service. If congregational songs are chosen, try to select familiar songs that are doctrinally sound, even though they might not be your first choice. You will want to provide words for the songs to help people participate. Some will still read the words, even if they don't know the tune or don't feel comfortable singing along.*

Scripture Readings

As mentioned in chapter 1, Scripture readings must be carefully chosen. In trying to be gospel-centered, you can never go wrong with passages that make the gospel clear in plain reading, such as Romans 5:6–11; 2 Corinthians 5:17–21; Ephesians 2:1–10. You will also want to read passages that will complement the main text of your sermon. For example, a great passage I've preached on at funerals is John 11, where Jesus raises Lazarus from the dead. A complementary—but not redundant—passage to read somewhere else in the service is the end of 1 Corinthians 15, where Christ takes the sting of death and gives us victory through him (verses 54–57), allowing us, as a consequence, to be steadfast and abounding in the work of the Lord until his return (verse 58). In services where you are confident of the deceased person's conversion,

---

* See appendix 3 for a list of suggested hymn selections.

passages that speak of the resurrection of our bodies to live eternally with Christ when he returns for his people are appropriate (1 Thessalonians 4:13–18), since they speak of a Christian's comfort when faced with death (verse 18).

Eulogy

In the North American context in which we minister, eulogies provide an opportunity for family and friends to acknowledge the deceased's contributions and achievements. However, great care must be taken to avoid eulogizing someone into heaven, especially when their life showed no fruit of genuine conversion. You want to guard against becoming so man-centered in your eulogy that the mourners are diverted from God and the gospel of grace. On the other hand, concern for these errors has left some ministers with a negative impression that causes them to avoid any use of eulogies. Our counsel is to avoid eulogizing the deceased if you think it will encumber clear preaching of the gospel.

What is a eulogy? The eulogy is the time in the service when your focus is on the person who has died. Even if you knew the deceased well, it is best to prepare the eulogy by having a meeting with the family, preferably when most of them are present. Typically, this can be done at the funeral home just before a session of visitation begins.* Spend time asking questions about the loved one—what they love and remember most about that person. Ask questions that provoke significant memories and reveal what they learned from the deceased and how their loved one served them. Ask about

---

* Don't forget to always have breath mints on you, as you will be talking closely to many different people at different times throughout the funeral process.

how their loved one was faithful as a spouse, parent, grandparent, soldier, employee/boss, neighbor, or friend. Also, listen for personality qualities that emerge about their loved one's sense of humor, compassion for others, leadership roles, and recreational activities. This template can be applied, no matter whether you are conducting a funeral of a Christian you knew well or a non-Christian you didn't know at all. The difference between these is in the way you weave the person's Christian testimony throughout each category. For a non-Christian, you can certainly talk about the person's life in an endearing way. They were a person created in the image of God — a person who loved, cared for, sacrificed, taught, and served their family and friends in their own way until the end.

This discussion with the family gives them an opportunity to talk about memories, share stories, and begin a healthy grieving process. We want people to grieve with hope because of Christ, but we must deal with the practical matters of instructing and helping them walk through the grieving process. A major aspect in grieving is learning to talk about the deceased through these stories and memories. This is a time for them to laugh, cry, remember, and celebrate the life of the one they loved. Again, this is essential for each of us as we learn to work through our grief. It's part of the work of pastorally caring for souls. To conclude the eulogy, a common practice is to read the obituary, which the funeral director will typically give to you on a minister's card.*

---

* A minister's card will have basic information that can function as a template to read for an obituary — date and place of birth and death, age, occupation, surviving family, church membership, etc.

Conduct Gospel-Centered Funerals

Sermon

The most helpful advice I ever received about preaching at a funeral for someone I didn't know was, "Don't preach them into heaven. Don't preach them into hell. Just preach the gospel for the people who are there." This principle captures the heart of your task in preaching, regardless of the unique details of the funeral itself. Ironically, though we spend the service remembering and celebrating the life of the deceased, the funeral service is ultimately not for them—it is for those who attend. This is why the sermon must include the gospel, which must be preached clearly. Only when we have confidence in a person's conversion should we feel comfortable speaking of the heavenly reward he or she has now received. If there is any doubt in your mind, it is best to keep the focus on the benefits of the gospel for your hearers, resisting the temptation to provide a false comfort that you have little or no basis to give.

As mentioned in chapter 1, a funeral sermon should not exceed twenty minutes. Most sermons should cover three topics, preferably expounding them from a text or collection of texts of Scripture. First, *acknowledge the need to grieve.* The story of the raising of Lazarus from the dead (John 11) is particularly helpful here. In this story there seems to be a legitimate time of grieving and sorrow for those who are experiencing the separation that death brings, including Jesus himself, who wept (John 11:35). I often share about the time my father sat down with my wife and me after learning that we had miscarried with our second child and told us to take some time to grieve over this child and instructed us in how to do so.* Don't assume that people know how to grieve. Some will believe grief is inappropriate. Some will not be able to work through their grief by simply *talking* about their deceased loved one. In actuality, many people do not want to talk because of the pain and hurt felt in the loss. Often, it isn't until years later that people learn the value of this process and eventually work through their grief with some pastoral guidance.

After acknowledging the need to grieve, *remind people that true hope in grief cannot come apart from the hope of the gospel.* Every funeral sermon should include a focus on Christ's person and work. Whatever text you choose to preach, make sure you are able to focus on the clear elements of the gospel—God's holiness, man's sinfulness and deserving judgment, Christ's perfect personhood and atoning work to save us, and our necessary response of repenting and believing in Christ.

After clearly communicating the gospel, the final topic of the sermon should *help those listening know how to respond to the gospel.* To do so appropriately and effectively, prepare by knowing as much as you can about your hearers as well as the deceased. You should assume both Christians *and* non-Christians are present. You should assume they have come with a preconceived understanding on how we receive eternal life. For example, I once did a funeral where 90 percent of those in attendance were devoted Catholics, another where the place was filled with Mormons, and another where no one in the

---

* How do you grieve over a child you didn't personally know? My father instructed us to spend time talking about the child in this way: Who would the child have looked like? Who would the child have acted like? How would the child have fit into our family?

building had ever stepped foot inside a church. In every case, I explained the gospel clearly, called my hearers to repent of their sins, believe in Christ, and trust in him. Yet each of these situations required a different approach to how I called them to respond to the gospel, depending on their preconceived understanding of the "good news."

In summary, exhort the attendees to grieve. Preach the gospel clearly and simply, helping them understand their need for Christ. And call them to repent and believe.

The Graveside Service

The graveside service involves traveling with the casket and with others to the grave site after the funeral. You will need to know what to *do* at the graveside and what to *say*. There are three aspects to the typical graveside service you will need to prepare for—the procession, the internment, and the words you share with the family after the service.

First comes the procession of the casket from the funeral home or church to the place where it will permanently rest. Your role as pastor is far from over after the funeral service is done. You are usually the one who leads the deceased to his or her final resting place. I remember feeling the immense weight of this responsibility at my first few funerals. Prepare for the procession by meeting with the funeral director. Inquire about the grave site's location and the duration of the drive. Find out if funeral home or cemetery personnel will be there to meet you at the cemetery and if anyone will direct you toward the appropriate grave site. This is a good time to decide if you wish to ride with the director or drive your own vehicle. When you first arrive at the funeral location, inform the director of your plan for the procession. Also, ask ahead of time where the casket will be loaded into the hearse so that you can be familiar with your surroundings. Since you will be involved in leading the casket from the funeral service to the hearse, you'll want to know where this will happen.

Second, you will want to prepare some short comments for the graveside internment service. Keep this brief—certainly not a full-length sermon. Have an introduction, a Scripture reading, and a prayer. Prepare a few words to share so that the entire service lasts no more than five to seven minutes. Remember that much has already been said and that this is a time of concluding the occasion and commending the body to the ground. Additionally, your comments may need to be extra brief in case someone else is speaking after you or you're dealing with the logistics of a military burial (something to add to your list to ask when meeting with the funeral director).

Your comments at the graveside will vary, depending on whether the deceased was a believer in Christ or not. For the Christian, you can remind people that the grave has been defeated. An appropriate exhortation to prepare for a Christian graveside is 1 Thessalonians 4:13–18, in which Paul addresses the resurrection of the physical body for those who are in Christ and whose bodies remain in the ground at the time of his return. After exhorting those gathered, prepare a final prayer in which the truth of that passage is understood for Christians and non-Christians who are present. For the funeral of a non-Christian or someone whose commitment to Christ was not clear, pick a passage that talks about the Lord's character and the way he comforts his people (Psalm 23, for example). Prepare a final prayer in which you point people to the way to be truly comforted by God and find hope in death through repentance and faith in the life, death, and resurrection of Jesus Christ. Make known the truth that the great Puritan John Flavel presented so powerfully: "O then, as you expect peace or rest in the chambers of death, get union with Christ. A grave with Christ is a comfortable place."[1]

Finally, you will want to prepare some comments of care for the family that you offer after the graveside service. Don't be in a rush to leave. You may say something during the funeral that the Lord will use to awaken someone to his or her need for Christ. Before leaving, approach the family. Offer your condolences. Have a card or some other information handy that you can give to the family or anyone else who asks to speak with you further. Finally, ask if there is any help you can give to the family in the future. They typically won't take you up on this offer, but the kind gesture and your willingness to help can be comforting to them. This leaves the door open for future ministry, whether or not they are church members.

The Prepared Pastor

Because there are so many elements to plan and logistics to prepare for, it is not uncommon for the pastor to have all his words prepared, the service planned out, everyone in place, the processional details checked off, and then realize that the most essential element has been neglected—himself. Do not become enslaved by the tyranny of funeral preparation only to get to the moment of the service and find that you are empty and drained and that your heart has grown calloused. Preparing for and conducting a funeral is an emotional and mental drain. Let me suggest three ways in which a pastor can take time to prepare his heart, mind, and soul.

Prepare for the unexpected. Just when you think you have seen it all, the next funeral will surprise you. You may have seen fights break out, arrests made, uncontrollable wailing, family members and pallbearers fainting, caskets dropped and knocked over, shouting matches between the family and funeral director, or funeral attire that would make most people blush, but that doesn't mean the next funeral will not be a fresh, new experience. Be prepared to see *anything.* You may get the craziest response to something you say. Prepare to watch families at their worst. If you expect something unexpected to happen, you will be able to think clearly and respond wisely when it happens.

Prepare to minister God's word. Though there is much to manage, administrate, and facilitate, you are not the concierge of the funeral. You are a minister of God's word and a preacher of the gospel of Jesus Christ. Prepare your heart, mind, and soul however you must, so that when you stand before people at the beginning of a funeral service, you stand to minister God's word, trusting that God will work mightily through his word.

Prepare to extend the hope of Christ. You are also not there to solve family conflicts or to help the funeral home learn how to function more smoothly. You are there to clearly present to each person the hope we have for victory over sin and death because of Christ. You can best prepare by thinking in advance about who will likely be at the funeral service. Consider what kinds of questions you want to ask the family to discover their spiritual condition when you talk with them. Prepare these questions ahead of time from the words you've prepared to share, so that gospel opportunities will show themselves in your conversations.

Wearing your administrator and facilitator cap throughout the process is necessary. You will need to maneuver through many details and demands. Nevertheless, remember that you are ultimately a pastor and evangelist who is called on by the Chief Shepherd to prepare and conduct funerals of dead men. Speak as "a dying man preaching to dying men."[2]

CHAPTER 3

PREACH

Phil Newton

What shall I say? A holy and good God has covered us with a dark cloud. O that we may kiss the rod, and lay our hands on our mouths! The Lord has done it.

> Sarah Edwards, in a letter to her daughter after the death of her husband, Jonathan Edwards

FUNERAL SERMONS (sometimes called homilies) tend to be briefer than a typical Sunday morning exposition of Scripture. At a funeral you are preaching to a mixed audience that may be unfamiliar with even the basics of the Christian faith. Simplicity and clarity must characterize your preaching. However, this does not mean you should avoid biblical doctrine or gospel application.

In This Chapter

- Focusing on the unchangeable character of God...
- Maintaining gospel clarity at the funeral...
- Understanding and preparing different types of funeral sermons...

Conduct Gospel-Centered Funerals

Funeral Sermon Essentials

In this chapter, we will consider a few key things to focus on in a funeral sermon.

The Unchangeable Character of God

Death does not change God. When a family loses a loved one, they may feel as if the world has collapsed. They will need the calm assurance that God is still on his throne and still at work in their time of need. Often, I read Psalm 46 to a grieving family or use it as my text for the sermon. This psalm pictures several cataclysmic upheavals in nature, among governments, and with people. In each scene, the Lord is found to be "our refuge and strength, an ever-present help in trouble" (Psalm 46:1).

When someone dies, something happens to the psyche of the survivors. They are brought, sometimes suddenly, face-to-face with loss. Death upsets the regular patterns of life. For some, life without their loved one seems unbearable. Acknowledge the pain of their loss and offer comfort, but make sure you also turn their attention to the greater reality—that the living God remains unchanging in this tumultuous world.

So my suggestion is to begin with the psalms. Like nowhere else in Scripture, the psalms consistently show us God's character in the midst of our troubling circumstances. For instance, Psalm 2 declares the Lord's reign over the nations and his unflinching steadiness in the face of opposition from the world's great powers. Psalms 3–4 offer prayers for morning and evening, encouraging us to put our trust in the Lord. Even when adversaries exclaim that our God cannot deliver us, the psalmist confidently affirms this:

But you, LORD, are a shield around me,
>   my glory, the One who lifts my head high...
Know that the LORD has set apart his faithful servant for
>   himself;
>   the LORD hears when I call to him.
Tremble and do not sin;
>   when you are on your beds,
>   search your hearts and be silent.
Offer the sacrifices of the righteous
>   and trust in the LORD.

Psalms 3:3; 4:3 – 5

Consider reading to grieving family members selections from Psalms 13, 18 – 19, 23 – 25, 27 – 28, 31, 33 – 34, 37, 40, 42 – 43, and others that are meaningful to you in your study. As you read, call attention to particular attributes of God's character that will help listeners focus on the Lord God as their strength and sufficiency.

In addition, you can read or tell the stories from biblical narratives of those going through suffering, trials, and adversity. Who cannot stop to marvel at God's providence with Joseph or his care of David or his sustaining strength for Daniel? Paul wrote that "we always carry around in our body the death of Jesus, so that the life of Jesus may also be revealed in our body" (2 Corinthians 4:10). "Though outwardly we are wasting away," declares Paul, "yet inwardly we are being renewed day by day" (verse 16). He could focus on the "eternal house in heaven" after giving up his confidence in the "earthly tent" of his body (2 Corinthians 5:1 – 4). In all these statements, Paul was expressing the dependability of God in any and every circumstance.

Conduct Gospel-Centered Funerals

When the deceased has given clear evidence that he or she was a faithful Christian, you will have almost limitless material to consider for your sermon as you talk with the family. You can point people to the promise of the resurrection of the dead (1 Corinthians 15) or the eternal dwelling prepared by Christ (John 14) or the indescribable wonder of the future state with Christ in heaven (Revelation 21 – 22). If there were no clear signs that the deceased followed Christ, then you will want to focus on the family's need, encouraging them to look to Christ in their need and sorrow. Direct their attention to the trustworthiness of God in comforting those who are troubled since he is the "God of all comfort" (2 Corinthians 1:3).

Clarity of the Gospel

A gospel minister never wants to sound an unclear note when communicating the gospel message. Your life and ministry should center on the gospel of Jesus Christ. So it is only appropriate that the focus of your ministry to the grieving offers them a wide spectrum of gospel applications. By this, I am saying that much like the multiple facets of the diamond will reflect beauty when held to the light, so the minister's conversation, prayers, Scripture readings, and presence will provide refractions of the gospel.

One of the most difficult questions a minister will face at this time may come from a grieving parent or child: "Is my loved one in heaven with Jesus?" Rather than assuming the position of eternal judge and offering a definitive answer to this question, point them to the Scriptures. Here you have an opportunity to apply the gospel. "My dear friend, Jesus Christ came to save lost sinners (Luke 19:10; 1 Timothy 1:15). He laid down his life, bearing our sin before the wrath of God, so that sinners like us might be set free and have the sweet assurance of relationship to him (Romans 5:9; Hebrews 2:14–18). The promise of God is that all the Father has given to Jesus come to him, and those who come to him he never drives away (John 6:37). To know him is to have eternal life (John 17:3). Your loved one's reliance on Jesus Christ in the gospel is the certainty of his eternal home."

A Call to Respond

Charles Haddon Spurgeon reminded his students, "The grand object of the Christian ministry is the glory of God. Whether souls are converted or not, if Jesus Christ be faithfully preached, the minister has not laboured in vain, for he is a sweet savour unto God as well in them that perish as in them that are saved." Yet, in typical Spurgeon fashion, he did not leave out the need to press the gospel: "Yet, as a rule, God has sent us to preach in order that through the gospel of Jesus Christ the sons of men may be reconciled to him ... The glory of God being our chief object, we aim at it by seeking the edification of saints and the salvation of sinners."[3]

Funerals are an opportunity to speak to an unbeliever's need for Christ as Savior and Lord. Clarify the gospel during the funeral sermon, presuming nothing, while calling for the hearers to give attention to their eternal condition. Make yourself available after the funeral or in the days afterward to meet with any who would like to discuss the gospel and talk about their spiritual need. Relationships established at a funeral service may bear fruit years later as an attendee begins to take seriously the call of the gospel. Faithful ministers sow the gospel seeds in such times and pray for God to make it grow.

Exhortation to Grieve

Grief is a *gift* from God to humanity. It is a gift because it allows us to express the emotional buildup that naturally accompanies deep loss. God created us as relational beings, so it is normal to grieve when separation comes. Death is not the way it is supposed to be — it is a result of human sin and a consequence of the fall.

Yet the Christian perspective on grief is different from other perspectives. Paul exhorted the Thessalonian church to grieve, yet not in the same way as the world grieves (1 Thessalonians 4:13). We know that grief is appropriate — even our Lord grieved at the grave of his close friend, Lazarus (John 11:35). But while the world grieves in confusion and without hope for the future, we grieve with hope. This distinction visibly separated Christians from non-Christians in the ancient Roman world. The Roman world characteristically grieved with hopelessness at the death of a loved one. One of the ancient writers put it this way: "Hopes are for the living; the dead are without hope."[4]

Ultimately, the struggle to grieve with hope requires us to grasp the promise God offers in the bodily resurrection, a promise that is ours because of the resurrection of Jesus Christ from the dead. Connecting the gospel to grief through the promise of the resurrection puts a different perspective on death from the one that the world offers. Ministers should encourage grief, but exhort people to grieve appropriately at the death of a Christian believer, knowing that they have eternal hope in Jesus Christ (John 14; 1 Corinthians 15). Augustine expressed this beautifully when he wrote:

> And you should not grieve as the heathen do who have no hope, because we have hope, based on the most assured promise, that as we have not lost our dear ones who have departed from this life but have merely sent them ahead of us, so we also shall depart and shall come to that life where, more than ever, their dearness to us will be proportional to the closeness we shared on earth and where we shall love them without fear of parting.[5]

Different Types of Sermons

As you prepare your sermon, you should consider the circumstances of the deceased's life and relationships. I have attended several funerals where it was quite obvious that the minister did not know the deceased. There is nothing wrong with this, of course. You may be asked to perform a funeral for someone you have never met, and that is perfectly acceptable. But you don't want to come across as uninterested or insensitive. Even when you knew the deceased well, you will want to pay close attention to the story of their life, to the unique ways in which their life circumstances intersected with the lives of others.

There are several typical situations you are likely to encounter. Here are some suggestions to help you appropriately weave the details of the person's life into your message.

Death of a Faithful Church Member

In one of my early pastorates, the life of an elderly woman who had been faithful to Christ and the church was slowly ebbing away. I visited her in the intensive care unit, and she haltingly spoke to me, showing appreciation for my visits and prayers. In my last visit with her, just a couple of hours before her death, she seemed to increase in her joy! She spoke of how she anticipated seeing the Lord Jesus and being welcomed into his presence. Her funeral service was not difficult to lead, for she had shown faithfulness for many years as a follower of Jesus Christ. My primary responsibility on this occasion was to celebrate the source of her joy by pointing the family to the promises of the gospel (e.g., John 3:16 – 18; 6:35 – 40; 14:1 – 7; Romans 8:18 – 39; 1 Corinthians 15:50 – 58). It also served as a wonderful occasion to remind her fellow church members of our corporate responsibilities in the kingdom of God.

Death of a Known Unbeliever

Ministers are occasionally asked to conduct funeral services for an unbelieving person. I believe we should be willing to do this for the sake of Christ and the gospel. In such cases, our responsibility is not to offer a declaration regarding the deceased's eternal destiny; it is to clearly proclaim the gospel. The only comfort for family members will be found in *their* response to the gospel of Jesus Christ. You can never fully predict or anticipate the impact of your preaching on occasions like this.

I was once asked to conduct a funeral for a man who had died of a drug overdose. He had never given any evidence of knowing Christ, although in recent years his sister had come to faith in Christ through our church's witness. The assembly that morning mirrored the relationships the man had had in his final years, and many of the people at the funeral did not know Christ. One pallbearer, in particular, caught my eye. It was wintertime and quite cold outside. A rough lifestyle etched this man's face. He was wearing blue jeans and a white T-shirt, and he had a pack of cigarettes rolled up in his sleeve. It was very cold at the graveside, but he seemed oblivious to the temperature. He had likely consumed enough alcohol or drugs that morning to assuage any consciousness of the cold. I felt a great burden as I spoke, for I knew that any number of those gathered could be the *next* one to overdose and die. I spoke that morning on the brevity of life and the reality of eternity.

Here are several things to consider when you conduct funerals for unbelievers:

1. Seek to serve the unbeliever's family. They may be resistant to gospel ministry, so you may have to gently but firmly explain your approach to funerals. Keep in mind that if you have been asked to conduct the funeral, you will carry it out as a minister of the gospel and not as a professional eulogizer. Also, look for ways that the church might be involved in ministry. Ask others in the church to join you in meeting with the deceased's family.

2. Find out what you can about the deceased's interests. If you can do so appropriately, relate some of these things in the funeral sermon. Although not a believer, he or she is created in the image of God (Genesis 1:26). Respect the dignity of personhood as you speak of him or her.

3. Keep your funeral message simple. Focus on the gospel. I recommend doing a simple exposition focusing on a narrative that helps the deceased's family and friends to visualize the gospel message. You could tell the story of Jesus raising Lazarus from the dead, while focusing on the doctrinal implications that are clear in the text (John 11). Or you could tell the

story of Nicodemus, who came to Jesus at night, showing how Jesus cut through the facade of Nicodemus's initial comments to get to the heart of the matter (John 3). Or tell the story of the rich young ruler who wanted to know how he could have eternal life, showing how Jesus stripped away for eternity all human dependency (Matthew 19:16–22).

4. Communicate the urgency of the moment while calling on hearers to consider the crucified and risen Lord Jesus Christ. It is certainly appropriate to let attendees know that you are available later in the day to talk about eternal issues if they so desire.

5. Look for opportunities to continue building relationships with the deceased's family and friends. Some may surprise you and show up for worship on a Sunday! Others, more likely, will have warm feelings toward you for taking the time to talk with them, even though they have shown no interest in the gospel or the church.

6. Continue praying for gospel fruit.

Death of a Child or Infant

Few occasions in ministry are more difficult than the death of a child or infant. One can only hope that you will rarely need to face these gut-wrenching times, but reality suggests otherwise. I still vividly remember the funeral service of a friend who was just two years older than me who died during my junior high years. He had suffered from a rare congenital issue that suddenly escalated right after a group of children from our church had gone on a daylong outing. We returned on a Saturday evening, and he died that next afternoon. The church auditorium was packed for the funeral service. His immediate and extended family filled several pews just in front of the open casket. I can still hear the sobs from that day. Sadly, the minister lacked a clear gospel focus in the service, offering little real hope to those gathered to mourn.

A few years ago, our church welcomed the birth of a precious little boy to one of our faithful families. They brought him to church just four weeks after his birth. He was a beautiful baby who seemed to enjoy the attention shown by his new church family. Yet just a few days afterward, the parents called to let us know that their son had been rushed to the hospital, listless and weak. He had no appetite and did not respond to stimulus. Over the next three months, he remained connected to life support at a local children's hospital. The medical staff fell in love with the little fellow, just as we all had. Their gallant efforts proved futile, as an undetected birth defect hastened his death. I joined the family in grieving over his departure. I learned much from those very difficult days about ministering to those who have lost a child or infant. Several years later, those lessons hit home as I found myself grieving the death of my granddaughter, who died only thirty minutes after her birth.

Here are several important things to remember in this situation:

1. Spend time with the family. This sounds simple enough, but busy schedules often keep us from being where we are most needed.

2. Listen to the family as they open their hearts and express their anguish. Do not try to immediately correct a comment or something they ask or say. Place yourself in their position — you might be saying the same thing. At an appropriate opportunity, gently offer correction through the authority of Scripture.

3. Read Scripture, especially passages about Jesus Christ and the sufficiency of his redemptive work. Talk about the texts you've read. In all likelihood, the family has missed being at corporate worship due to caring for their dying child, so bring the ministry of the word to them.

4. Pass along an appropriate booklet or book or copy of material you believe would offer encouragement. Stories in the lives of William Carey, Adoniram Judson, or others may prove to be an encouragement as you relate how they handled the loss of their children.[6]

5. Be present in an unhurried manner. You may have a busy schedule, but it is imperative that you do not rush in and out during these times of pastoral care. Give priority to grieving family members' needs, praying for them and ministering the gospel to them.

6. At the funeral service, bring to the surface some of the truths you have talked about in previous days. Let the word of God speak with power and clarity.

"Early Death" through Disease or Accident

Particularly in the West, we live with a sense of divine right that we should live to a ripe old age. Those who live in the rest of the world know this is an illusion. They are familiar with the harsh realities of life and the likelihood of dying an "early death," whether by disease, recurring natural disasters, or war. Since we minister among people who live in a culture that knows little of this adverse reality, we must be prepared to bring comfort and truth during situations when death comes quickly and unexpectedly early.

Even though I was no stranger to death, having worked

with my dad at the funeral home in my youth, my first experience as a pastor came at the funeral of a twenty-four-year-old mother. She had just returned home after giving birth to her first child. There was all the normal excitement associated with a birth until she noticed a distinct discoloration of her skin. A trip to the doctor landed her immediately in the hospital for tests, leaving her two-week-old baby at home. The diagnosis was grim—a rapidly growing tumor on her liver that left her with only a few months to live.

My family and I were on our way out of town when we received the call letting us know what had happened, so we quickly returned home. I remember going to my study and praying on my knees over the Bible, hoping to have something to share with this family at the time of their need. I visited her and, to my complete surprise, found her radiant with joy in the Lord. Instead of ministering to her, she ministered to my downcast heart! Over the next three months, I visited with her and her husband many times, reading Scripture, praying, and talking. I pleaded with the Lord to heal her. I still remember the phone call in the middle of the night, as the husband told me that his wife had just died.

Here are some of the things I learned through this experience:

1. Spend time with the family.

2. Talk about the providence of God. Walk through biblical stories that illustrate the providence of God at work in every situation (e.g., Joseph, Job, Daniel, and Paul). Avoid quick pronouncements or simplistic statements such as "God's will is that your child die young." Even if it is true (theologically), it will take time for grieving family members and friends

to work through their pain and questions and learn to rest in the wisdom and purpose of God in their loss.

3. Focus on the gospel and eternity. Talk about the life of Jesus Christ and how he, too, died an "early death" on our behalf. Look at Paul's desire to be with Christ, which he considered "better by far" (Philippians 1:23). Talk about heaven and all that Jesus has promised for his followers (John 14:1 – 3; Revelation 21 – 22).

4. For the funeral service, avoid offering a theodicy that justifies God's timing in taking this life. Focus instead on the wisdom of God's providence in all things. Here you will need to be strong in speaking doctrinal truth while avoiding complicated reasoning. Simply state the truths of providence and illustrate them biblically. Explain how early deaths do come for believers and unbelievers alike. Then make the point that a believer in Christ is the one best prepared for a sudden death.

5. Look for opportunities to minister to family and friends in the days following the funeral.

Death by Suicide

Nothing jars the mind and the emotions like news of a suicide. I remember how shocked I felt when I returned home for a visit during my sophomore year in college to learn that the father of one of my close friends had committed suicide. I asked my dad, "Why did he do it?" His reply has stuck with me to this day: "Why does anyone take his own life?" My dad let me know that we could conjure up all kinds of ideas but that ultimately no one knows the answer to that question. I think that is wise advice. Don't try to answer the question or speak to the motive of the person in this situation. So, then, what *does* the gospel minister say in this situation?

Admit that no one knows exactly what is going on in the mind of a person who takes his or her own life. Avoid making quick judgments. Sometimes there are emotional illnesses or physiological conditions that can contribute to a snap decision to take one's life. John Newton, the famous Anglican minister and author of "Amazing Grace," spent years ministering to William Cowper, one of the eighteenth century's most beloved hymnists, during Cowper's struggles with depression, melancholy, and attempted suicide.[7] Realize that even devoted Christians struggle with these things.

As family members ask why, you can probe with them the rationale behind their loved one's decision (don't avoid it), but be careful not to dig too deeply at that emotionally charged point. Your goal is to help the family as they deal with the sense of guilt they will inevitably feel. In probing for a rationale, they are very likely trying to understand what part they might have had in the suicide. Here we must assure the family that the decision to take one's life rests with the deceased alone. Help them to be honest in their grief and guilt, but above all point them to the peace found in the gospel of Jesus Christ.

The funeral service is an opportunity to demonstrate biblically how the gospel is an anchor for us in the worst storms of life. The service is really about how the gospel applies in such settings, not a time for answering unanswerable questions about suicide or the state of the deceased.

Death of a Stranger

Although many people go through life with no interest in God, the gospel, or spiritual issues, when it comes time to die, they generally want a minister to conduct their funeral service.

Conduct Gospel-Centered Funerals

Consequently, ministers will be called on to conduct funeral services for complete strangers who may or may not have any relationship to them or to the members of their church. If you are facing a situation like this, you will want to meet with family members (if any are around) to gain as much information as possible about the deceased. You will probably have a good opportunity to talk about Christ and the gospel when you meet with the family. After the initial meeting, you may find the following considerations helpful:

1. Seek to discern if there was any interest in spiritual matters at some stage in the deceased's life. It could be that the stranger was in a nursing home but previously showed faithfulness as a Christian. You may want to refer to this during the funeral.

2. Cultivate relationships with the family members (assuming family members are somewhere in the area). Read Scripture and pray when visiting with them. Ask about specific ways that you and your congregation might serve them. Encourage them to join you for worship on any subsequent Sundays.

3. At the funeral, if knowledge of the deceased is limited, use the funeral card or minister's card from the funeral home to sketch together information about the deceased's birthplace, education, family, career, etc. This could be useful early in the service.

For instance, you might say something like this: "We gather this morning to remember Jane Smith, who was born in Chicago and spent most of her life in Memphis. She attended school locally and worked for many years as a receptionist at Community Medical Center. Ms. Smith is survived by nieces and nephews who have expressed appreciation for her attentiveness to them during their adolescence. Family members remember with fondness her warm smile, dependable birthday cards, and the wonderful chocolate cakes she brought to family gatherings. For the past twenty years, Ms. Smith was a resident of Community Nursing Home. She passed away last Thursday at the age of ninety." Your goal here is to give the service a personal touch, even though the individual is unknown to you.

You may want to be candid with those at the service and admit that you did not personally know the deceased. Some will immediately know this, so it alleviates some awkwardness in admitting it. You might say, "Although I never had the privilege of knowing Ms. Smith, the family asked me to speak to you today from God's word. It is through his word that we hear God speak to our needs during this time of grief." From that point on in the service, you can read the text of Scripture and expound and apply it as time allows.

4. Avoid general statements like "If Ms. Smith were here today, she would want me to tell you to do business with God" or "Ms. Smith would want you to know that a day of reckoning with God will come." Statements like this are an attempt to gain emotional empathy with your hearers rather than depending on the living and abiding word of God to do its work (Hebrews 4:12).

5. Utilize your opportunity of conducting the funeral to make the gospel clear. Keep in mind that in circumstances like this, brevity is appropriate — and expected.

Death of a Relative

Over the years, I have spoken at a number of my relatives' funerals. I count this a privilege, since most have not been part of my regular church ministry. These occasions mark a solemn opportunity to speak the gospel to those I've long known. As a family member, I am privy to the serious spiritual issues those in attendance are dealing with. While I may be tempted to make specific application to those issues, I need to remember that my purpose as a gospel minister is to speak the gospel to those in need. Addressing secondary and tertiary matters in the family can wait for another time.

Because you as the pastor are a family member, you have detailed remembrances that can be alluded to in the funeral. However, be sure to avoid spending more time on remembrances than in sharing the gospel. On the other hand, certain stories can give a personal touch at the funeral and open hearts to the message by blunting the tension that often accompanies a funeral service.

If the family member gave testimony of knowing Christ, then pass along some of the conversations you had with him or her. Talk about the deceased's love of Christ, the gospel, and their church. Making mention of their service through the local church can encourage attendees.

If the minister thinks he cannot contain his emotions while conducting a close relative's service, then he need not feel guilty about passing the sermon along to a colleague. Ministers grieve too! The family will not be helped by a lengthy emotional release during a service. I struggled with this when I led funeral services for my dad, father-in-law, and mother-in-law. Being close to them, I had to work through some of my own grief before stepping into the pulpit. I had a few moments when I felt my heart would explode, but the Lord gave me grace to continue. Each service proved to be helpful to family and friends in attendance.

You will likely think of other funeral scenarios we haven't mentioned here. We realize that variety attends funerals! Our goal is simply to offer concrete ideas that can be implemented in various circumstances. Thoughtful reflection about the details of each funeral's uniqueness will allow for dependence on the Lord and a sense of freshness in ministering the gospel to grieving families and friends.

CHAPTER 4

PERFORM

Brian Croft

> Thus we spend our years with sighing: it is a valley of tears, but death is the funeral of all our sorrows.
>
> Thomas Watson, "A Believer's Privilege at Death"

YOU'VE PLANNED WISELY. You've prepared diligently. Yet just like a Sunday sermon in a busy week of ministry, a funeral can notoriously sneak up on you sooner than you realize. Regardless of whether you feel inadequate or well prepared, dependence on the Lord is essential. As you travel to the funeral home to be an ambassador of Christ, remember that you are there to make him central in all you are about to do.

There are three major categories to consider as you prepare to conduct a

In This Chapter

- Confirming the preservice and postservice details...
- Conducting the funeral service and graveside service...
- Caring for the family after the service...

funeral. Even though most of this has been mentioned in previous chapters, I want to focus here on specific items related to actually performing the funeral.

Preservice Details

Depending on the situation, arrive at the funeral home fifteen to thirty minutes before the funeral starts. This allows you to greet the family, check in with the funeral director, and ensure that plans haven't changed since the director last talked with you (because they often do change). This will also prevent one of the most embarrassing moments of your ministry — being late to conduct a funeral (trust me, I know). Inform the funeral director at this time whether you will ride with him to the graveside or drive on your own in the procession. Make sure those involved in the service are accounted for and have prepared what you have asked of them. It is ideal to gather others involved in the service a few minutes before starting in order to talk through the service and pray that the Lord would awaken souls to the gospel and comfort his hurting people. Finally, make sure you start on time. Many folks have come early in the anticipation that the service will start when announced. Though there are exceptions, you should be able to count on the funeral director to help make this happen and not to hinder it.

Some funeral homes close the casket before the service begins. In one tradition, the minister is typically asked to meet for prayer with the family prior to the beginning of the funeral service. Often, if the casket is already in the chapel, the director will close the casket prior to the family's entrance. In other traditions where the deceased has been lying in state in a family room, the minister will pray with the family and then the family will be led to the chapel. Meanwhile, the minister waits with the casket as the directors close it. Then he leads the casket into the service, motioning for the attendees to stand in honor of the deceased. What's important is not so much the specific tradition, but that you make sure you know the standard protocol for that particular funeral home. Don't assume all of them do things the same way.

Funeral Service

There is certainly much to think about as you perform this service. You have prepared a lot of material. You have heard many suggestions of what to do and how to do it. Stand firmly on your decisions. Facilitate the funeral, making sure Christ and his saving work are on display throughout it. Pray sympathetically. Speak the eulogy in the way you would want yourself to be remembered. Read God's word, knowing it is living, active, and sharper than any two-edged sword, capable of piercing the deepest parts of our being (Hebrews 4:12). Exhort those who grieve, knowing how helpful that counsel once was to you. Preach the gospel and call people to respond to it, because you know that faith comes by hearing the word of Christ (Romans 10:17). Then trust in God to do his mighty work by his Spirit according to his good and perfect will.

Postservice Details

There are several tasks remaining after the funeral service has come to an end. Some of these tasks pertain to the time before the funeral procession heads to the grave site; others will be performed at the graveside service; still others involve the pastoral care opportunities you may have at the grave site after the service has ended, as well as in caring for the family in the days and weeks after the funeral.

At the Funeral Home

Once you conclude the service, it is customary to stand at the head of the casket while the funeral director comes to dismiss the attendees and give direction. You will hear different advice on this matter, but I find it helpful to be positioned at the head of the casket to be available for those who would like to greet me, but not blocking the exit if they prefer otherwise. I once co-led a funeral with a pastor who at the conclusion of the service placed himself, not at the head of the casket, but at the center of the door by which everyone had to exit. As I stood at the head of the casket, I watched many awkward moments of which this pastor was sadly unaware. Don't be offended if someone seems to bypass you. Often the attendees are led to the front to greet the emotional family and then walk to the casket to say their own final good-bye. Don't be surprised if you are overlooked in the midst of that moment. However, you will have some who will want to greet you. Appear inviting. Speak warmly and kindly. Some of the most encouraging feedback I have heard after a funeral has been at that moment. Probably the most heartening thing I ever hear in such moments, having just concluded a funeral for a non-Christian, is when some unknown person approaches and says, "Thank you for preaching the gospel clearly."

After the attendees have been escorted outside the room, family members are given their final moment with their loved one before the casket is closed (assuming the casket is still open). Remain in the room, but move from the vicinity of the casket so the family can have their time and space. Your presence in that moment will often be a source of great encouragement to the family. In typical protocol, once the family has been escorted outside, the funeral director closes the door to the room in order to close the casket. This prevents any unnecessary trauma to the family, who might have a hard time watching the casket shut. You will stay for the closing of the casket as the overseer of the proceedings, as well as the one who leads the casket to the hearse that is waiting outside.

Once the funeral director gives you the signal, walk in front to lead the casket through the doors for the pallbearers to lift the casket into the hearse. You will then proceed to the front car to ride with the funeral director (which I recommend), or you will get in your own car, which typically will have been put in the proper position in the procession by a funeral home employee. If you ride with the director, you may be tempted to try to accomplish a few tasks in the slow, gentle journey to the grave site. However, take advantage of this time to build a relationship with the director.

At the Grave Site

Once you arrive at the grave site, walk to the back of the hearse, as you will be the one to lead the casket to the grave. In the same way you walked in front to lead the casket to the hearse, you walk in front to lead it to the grave. The grave site is typically marked with a canopy or some kind of visual cue that is easy to spot. However, if you have any doubts where to proceed, just ask the director. Be careful as you walk through the uneven ground and maneuver through the scattered graves to reach the open grave that awaits the deceased's body. You will again stand at the head of the casket once it has been placed on the lowering device that holds the casket above the prepared grave.

I am not a fan of lengthy graveside services. You have just conducted a full funeral. The family may well be on the edge of emotional exhaustion, and often the conditions at the grave site are less than ideal. The pastor's portion of the graveside service should last no longer than five minutes. Keep in mind that any military ceremony or additional graveside logistics will come after you and can be lengthy, depending on how decorated the deceased was.

Our aim at a graveside is to reiterate the hope we have in Christ that we preached at the funeral service. I typically find an introduction, a Scripture reading, and a final prayer reflecting on the passage to be an appropriate, tasteful, and time-sensitive approach to a graveside service. For the deceased whom you are confident was a believer in Christ, 1 Thessalonians 4:13–18 and 1 Corinthians 15:50–58 are fitting to read, serving as a wonderful opportunity to encourage and comfort fellow believers that this body being commended to the ground will one day be raised to forever be with Christ. For those whose spiritual state before passing away is less clear, reading a more general passage of comfort (Psalm 23) is appropriate. Use the final prayer as a way to drive home the spiritual reality that true comfort from God comes from trusting in the life, death, and resurrection of his Son. The funeral director will typically close the graveside service.

Postfuneral Pastoral Care Opportunities

Allow yourself time to mingle at the grave site for a few minutes. This may be the time someone asks you about something you said in the service. Don't underestimate how the Lord can provide gospel opportunities in these moments before you leave. Once you have made yourself available for a few moments, approach the immediate family members to pay your respects one last time. This will often provide an opportunity for them to say thank you for serving them through the service. Have a business card in hand, offer your care to them for any reason in the future, and ask if they need anything else from you before you leave.

Make a plan to touch base with the family within the next month to see how they are doing, especially if they are members of your church.[8] The grieving process takes time for everyone. Trust that the Lord has been at work through your words to them throughout the entire process. Once life returns to a more normal routine, the truths you spoke are more likely to begin to take root and bear fruit. Call the family. Meet with them. Ask them how they are doing. Ask them if they feel like they have been grieving—and are doing so with hope. Ask how Christ has been a comfort to them if they are Christians, or—if not—ask if they had considered your words about the gospel since the funeral. Ask if there is any way you can serve them now. Involve other church members in the postfuneral care, as the family will benefit greatly by being cared for by both the body of Christ and the pastor. Often, it will be in the weeks and even months that follow when the hard sowing of the gospel seed through the funeral process begins to bear fruit. Try to be there for the harvest.

Finally, say good-bye to the funeral director before leaving. Make sure you encourage him if he skillfully handled the details on his end and made the experience more enjoyable for you. Don't forget the director is serving this family with the same hope that they will feel cared for by his efforts. Offer your services to him in the future, since all funeral homes need pastors to fill in when other pastors are unavailable.

Regardless of where you find yourself in the process of conducting a funeral, do not overlook the many details that accompany them. These details can be difficult, even overwhelming, to think about. Yet it is essential to know them well and faithfully maneuver through them. How we educate ourselves on the challenges, logistics, and practicalities that come with funerals can determine if the platform we are given for the gospel is credible in the eyes of those we pray will find their hope in Christ in their darkest hour.

ACKNOWLEDGMENTS

Brian

My coauthor Phil should have been the sole author of this book. Phil grew up around a funeral home and was raised by a faithful father who worked as a funeral director and taught him to care for people dealing with the tragedy of death. Phil conducted his first funeral before I was even born, and he was in the trenches of pastoral ministry before I was potty trained. Needless to say, Phil has graciously allowed me to ride on his coattails by including me in this book. Allow me to say thank you to Phil for his kind, humble, and inclusive spirit.

I must confess that I found myself more excited to work with Phil, learn from a seasoned pastor, and have an excuse for us to fellowship together than I was to write another book. Yet I am grateful that in the Lord's kindness all those expectations were met, and we also completed the book—one we hope the Lord will use as a helpful, practical tool to assist pastors in ministering the gospel in some of the most opportune times of people's lives. I pray that you've benefited from Phil's wisdom and experience in reading this book half as much as I did in working on this project with him.

I also want to express my deep appreciation to Joe and Joey Ratterman, Charley, and the entire Ratterman Funeral Home for allowing me the opportunity to conduct so many funerals for them when a pastor was unavailable or unknown to a hurting family. In writing this book, I drew from the lessons I learned in those difficult, unique, and often unpredictable situations. By God's grace, I look forward to many years of future work together. Thank you for your investment, confidence, and friendship.

As always, my wife and children remained steadfast in love, patience, and support throughout this project. I dedicate my portion of the book to my father, Bill Croft, who as a physician exemplified care for both the dying and the families of those enduring the death of a loved one.

Phil

My coauthor Brian should have been the sole author of this book. In his other books, he has demonstrated a unique ability to help pastors serve their congregations and communities. Brian's blog, *Practical Shepherding*, is filled with the kind of down-to-earth, practical, biblical, and insightful material that I wish I'd had access to in the early years of my pastoral ministry.* It would have saved me from making a multitude of mistakes! In a word, Brian *connects*. He does not approach pastoral work as an "armchair pastor," telling others what to do but hardly lifting a finger to the task himself. He speaks as one who lives in the trenches of pastoral work. Anyone reading Brian finds his own pastoral understanding enriched.

Joining with a fellow pastor of kindred spirit to write a book that offers help to those ministering to grieving families is a longtime dream come true. I have wanted to write on this subject for years but have lacked someone who could

---

* Visit Brian's blog at www.practicalshepherding.com.

compensate for my obvious weaknesses. Brian is just that person. He sees details I tend to overlook. Having spent plenty of time counseling fellow pastors, Brian understands what pastors need. I hope you found his writing an aid in serving Christ and his church more faithfully.

I want to express my appreciation for my fellow elder Jim Carnes, who provided a recommended list of hymns to use at funeral services. A special thanks goes to Mike Nowlin, Matt Sliger, and Rich Shadden for their editing assistance. Also, I express my deep affection and appreciation for Randy and Stacey McLendon, Chuck and Suzanne Buchanan, and Chris and Jessica Wilbanks. Their losses of Jackson McLendon, Peyton Buchanan, and Jordan Wilbanks taught me much about resting in the sufficiency of Christ in the face of death. As always, my wife, Karen, has been an encouragement to me as I worked on this manuscript. I dedicate my portion of this book to the memory of my father, Joe E. Newton (1925 – 1998), who exemplified compassionate care for those enduring the death of a loved one.

EXAMPLES OF FUNERAL SERMONS

Phil Newton

Meditation on the Words of Christ*

John 14:1–6

On the eve of his death, Jesus Christ spoke to his disciples the most comforting words found in Scripture. We turn to his words—for in them we find life, hope, peace, comfort, and clarity as we grieve at the death of _____. It is right for us to grieve and to have sorrow, yet not as those who have no hope. Even Jesus wept at the death of his dear friend Lazarus; so our Lord understands the heaviness you feel during this time. Yet, with this understanding also comes the promise and certainty of Christ through the gospel. Consider with me the words of Jesus Christ just before he went to the cross to bear our sins and open the way to the Father.

A. "Do not let your heart be troubled" (literally, "Stop letting your heart be troubled")

Is that a cruel, uncompassionate command to those weighed down with grief? Indeed, Jesus' disciples felt a heaviness of

---

* This sermon was used at the funeral of an infant but can be easily adapted for other funeral services. Note that the Scripture used in this message is taken from the NASB.

grief when they heard his words. He, as the Man of Sorrows acquainted with grief, understands grief as evidenced by his sorrow at the news of Lazarus's death and as Jesus visited the tomb.

1. Remember the context.

Jesus' declaration of his departure brought sorrow to the disciples. They could not see and grasp the future glory that this departure through death and resurrection would bring. Peter's denial of Christ had been foretold. Imagine the stunned looks when they realized that their own "rock," Simon Peter, would be exposed as weak and helpless (John 13:36–38).

2. Observe a few considerations.

It is normal to be focused on the momentary, the present — that's where the disciples were in their emotions and thoughts. But it is not always healthy to remain there.

It is normal to be absorbed with those things most dear to us — thus we see the disciples absorbed with Christ. And it is normal to be absorbed by the most pressing matters before our eyes — thus the disciples could only think of keeping Jesus with them. These are normal things, but not always best.

It is normal to think that a deep grief or pain or sorrow will *never* go away. Yet *never* is a long time, and we are not lord of that time or of God's wise and kind purpose in it.

3. Listen to the command.

So Jesus, recognizing that his disciples were already troubled, with great compassion and wisdom, told them it was time to no longer be troubled. They had gone through the ripping emotions of thinking they would never see him again. But he directs them to something much greater, something lasting and eternal — being in his Father's house.

B. Why we can bring troubled hearts to rest and peace—
two commands from Christ

1. "Believe in God."

Believe in God—not a god of your imagination or your superstitions or your design.

Believe in God—the God of Holy Scripture, the Father of our Lord Jesus Christ, the maker of heaven and earth, the owner of the cattle on a thousand hills, the One to whom the heavens and earth belong.

Believe in God—the One who has given names to all of the stars, the One who knows when a sparrow falls and who knows the very hairs on your head.

Believe in God—the One who dwells in unapproachable light, whom no man has seen or can see, who gives life and breath and existence to all things.

Believe in God—the One who is our refuge and strength and who is an ever-present help in time of need, the One who is our light and salvation before whom the nations are but a drop in the bucket and a speck of dust on the scales, who is our shepherd who comforts us with his rod and staff and who prepares a table before us in the presence of our enemies.

Believe in God—the One who has elected a people in Christ before the foundation of the world, who did not spare his own Son but delivered him over for us all, and who freely gives us all things in Christ Jesus.

Believe in that God! Ponder his infinite majesty, goodness, loving-kindness, wisdom, mercy, and love. Ponder how he sent his Son on your behalf.

"Do not let your heart be troubled," Jesus said. Yes, *believe in God*—what a God he is to soothe troubled hearts.

2. *"Believe also in Me."*

Again, we are not to believe in a Jesus of sentimentalism or a Jesus of our fanciful imagination, but Jesus Christ the Lord revealed in Holy Scripture, the only unique Son of God the Father, who is coequal with the Father, who possesses all of the divine attributes.

Believe in Jesus Christ, who is eternal and immortal, who himself made everything and apart from him nothing has come into being, who in the fullness of time was sent by the Father to be conceived by the Holy Spirit in the virgin's womb, who was born under the Law so that he might redeem those under bondage to the Law.

Believe in Jesus Christ, who lived a sinless life though tempted in all things as we are, who is therefore a merciful and faithful high priest knowing our weaknesses.

Believe in Jesus Christ, who preached the gospel of the kingdom, who healed the sick, gave sight to the blind, raised the dead, and welcomed little children to himself, held them in his arms, and blessed them, saying, "Of such is the kingdom of God."

Believe in Jesus Christ, who fulfilled all righteousness, in whom all the fullness of the Godhead dwells bodily, who willingly laid down his life as our redeemer to satisfy God as a propitiation with reference to our sins, who absorbed the Father's wrath through his bloody death on the cross.

Believe in Jesus Christ, who cried in triumph on the cross, "It is finished!" Who was buried in a borrowed tomb and three days later was raised by the glory of the Father, who ascended to the right hand of the Father, waiting for that time when the last enemy — death — will be made a footstool for his feet.

Believe in Jesus Christ, who continues as our Great High Priest, who rules in sovereign majesty, who will gather his church as his bride, who will judge the living and the dead.

This One is so full of glory, honor, majesty, and power that we know him by many titles because none fully express his fullness and accomplishments: Son of God, Son of Man, Messiah, King of kings, Lord of lords, the Good Shepherd, the Light, the Door, the Way, the Truth, the Life, the Word, the Lion of the tribe of Judah, the Lamb, the Alpha and the Omega, the Great God and Savior, Christ Jesus our Lord — believe in him.

"Believe also in Me," says Jesus, and in so believing, "Do not let your heart be troubled."

C. *The assurance of Christ for all who belong to him*

1. The Father has a big house with lots of rooms.

The picture given is that of an endless, sprawling mansion or palace unrivaled by all of the mansions of the world combined, with each place specially prepared for those who will dwell there.

It is the place where the Father and Son dwell. Its foundation is of precious stones; its gates of pearls; its streets of translucent gold. There's no need of sun or moon to shine there, for the glory of God and the Lamb illumines it.

2. Jesus has gone ahead of us to prepare a place for all whom he has redeemed through the purchase of his atoning death.

Not one of those whom Christ has secured through his death will be missing. There's room in the Father's house for all whom Christ died to save. None elected by sovereign grace before the foundation of the world and consequently redeemed by the price of Christ's bloody death will be absent from the Father's house. Jesus himself prepares a place for us. Every room is furnished with perfect love and peace. No sorrow or death or tears or pain or illness or disease or syndrome or war or heartache will find a place there. The Lamb makes sure of that!

3. Jesus will bring us to his home.

Some Jesus brings earlier than others. Some he spares the sorrows of this world by securing them out of his sovereign grace through his redemptive death and bringing them to his home while they are infants. The Anglican hymn writer and minister John Newton wrote to console some close friends whose infant had died, "I hope you are both well reconciled to the death of your child. I cannot be sorry for the death of infants. How many storms do they escape! Nor can I doubt, in my private judgment, that they are included in the election of grace." Charles Haddon Spurgeon consoled those in his own congregation in London: "Now, let every mother and father here present know assuredly that it is well with the child, if God hath taken it away from you in its infant days."9

Can we who live so few years in this life deny the eternal joys given by Christ to those little ones he takes early to his home? Yes, we struggle with the temporal loss we feel. Yes, we grieve at the thought of the few years of this life cut short. Yet something far more wonderful than we can offer with the best of our love and care has been given to this precious little one by Jesus Christ.

Do not let your heart be troubled.
Believe in God.
Believe in Jesus Christ.

Trust Christ's wisdom, love, purpose, and promise. He takes care of those whom he brings to the Father's house.

The way to the Father — the way to his eternal home of perfect holiness, infinite love, and divine glory — is found in Christ alone. "I am the way, and the truth, and the life; no one comes to the Father but through Me."

An Anchor in Stormy Times*
Hebrews 6:13–20

Facing the death of a friend or loved one is never an easy matter. Even when death follows a long life or terminal illness, there are still deep emotions and puzzling questions that cloud our thoughts. Yet this is especially difficult when the circumstances of someone's death pass beyond the grasp of our reasoning abilities. My friend _____'s death fits such a picture. Why at such a promising age and stage of life would _____ leave us abruptly? I confess that this question goes beyond our grasp. So my purpose is not to grapple with the perplexing whys that bring us together. Rather, I want us to consider a few things that are sure and certain, so that our confidence will not be found in ourselves or in our reasoning but in the eternal sufficiency of Jesus Christ.

I would turn our attention to a portion of God's word in the epistle to the Hebrews. This book was written during a very trying time in the early church. Believers, young and old, struggled with the future and the present. They lived in dangerous times, with the maniacal emperor Nero unleashing intense persecution against Christians. These believers wrestled with how to continue in an open display of their faith in Christ. Many were weary, sagging in their faithfulness and distraught over the anxieties they faced. Could they go on? On top of this, serious doctrinal errors had crept in among

---

* This sermon was preached at the funeral of a young man who had committed suicide. I'm indebted to my dear friend Ray Pritchard for helpful thoughts that I've incorporated into this message. Note that the Scripture used in this message is taken from the NASB.

them, eroding their spiritual foundation. The errors put the weight of their eternity on the level of their performance and on adherence to certain religious rituals instead of on Christ. These were weak, desperate people. They did not have much confidence about the days ahead.

It is in this setting that we read these words from Hebrews 6. *(Read verses 13–20.)*

Using the background of God's promise and oath to Abraham at the difficult time when his future seemed bleak, the writer of Hebrews makes some assertions that apply to the early Christians and to all who have taken refuge in Jesus Christ. *We discover that a Christian is one who has taken refuge in Jesus Christ in his sufficiency as Savior and King.* How does this passage apply to each of us?

1. Christians can become extremely weak and in dire need of encouragement.

We sometimes get the idea in popular Christianity that being a Christian means you always have your act together, that you are always full of smiles and confidence. If this were so, then no Christian would ever need the encouragement of our text, along with many other passages in God's word.

Sometimes even the best and seemingly most mature among us get *confused and lose our way.* It is as though a cloud of black darkness overshadows the light in which we've joyfully walked. In such times we may *temporarily lose sight of the Lord.* Like the psalmist who cried to the Lord, "Why have You forgotten me? Why do I go mourning because of the oppression of the enemy?" (Psalm 42:9), the believer cries out in desperation. Our eyes seem incapable of focusing on the Lord; our minds become insensitive to the promises of his presence. We feel alone, helpless, and without hope.

Although we may temporarily lose sight of the Lord, *he does not lose sight of us.* Thus we find simple encouragement in such times in verses 17 – 18 of Hebrews 6. The encouragement of God's faithfulness and the certainty of his promises in the gospel lead us "to take hold of the hope set before us." All who have taken refuge in Jesus Christ and the eternal provision of forgiveness and righteousness through his death and resurrection are to find strength in contemplating God's faithfulness and the surety of his promises in Christ.

So take hold of this "hope." The author of Hebrews calls it "the hope"—not a word of wishful thinking, as we are accustomed to using it—but "the hope" or confident expectation that Jesus Christ has conquered sin and death on our behalf, and has secured a place for us in heaven for all eternity. This hope belongs only to those who have found the refuge of faith in Christ alone.

2. Hope in Christ serves to anchor us in the most calamitous storms of life.

The biblical use of hope pictures something that is sure and certain but something that we've not yet physically touched—it remains before us as a future expectation. The eternal promises through Christ constitute this hope or anticipation of being in Christ's presence for all eternity. The weakest times a Christian faces are those days when his hope is unsettled and a cloud of darkness sits heavily above him. And so this New Testament writer reminds us to be diligent in coming back to the reality of "the full assurance of hope" (Hebrews 6:11).

But we sometimes falter, don't we? We are squeezed and shaken by things outside of our control. We are buffeted by our own personal weaknesses, sins, and twists of personality. So what must we do? We must take a fresh look at Jesus Christ and what he accomplished with finality on the cross. Our text calls this "an anchor of the soul" (verse 19).

What is the purpose of an anchor? It steadies us and keeps us secure from drifting or being tossed about by rough seas. If your hope is in Christ, then you have this anchor of the soul. Take note of it. It is "sure" — it is completely reliable to carry us through every vexing storm of life and into eternity. Paul expressed it best in the immortal words of Romans 8:38–39: "For I am convinced that neither death, nor life, nor angels, nor principalities, nor things present, nor things to come, nor powers, nor height, nor depth, nor any other created thing, will be able to separate us from the love of God, which is in Christ Jesus our Lord."

It is "steadfast" — there's no weakness or deceit or wavering in what Christ has accomplished for us. And it is a hope "which enters within the veil." This picture alludes to the shadow of the high priest entering the Holy of Holies each year to atone for the people's sins. But here, it is no earthly tabernacle and mercy seat that must have a yearly sacrifice, but rather a heavenly one. The anchor is securely fixed upon the sufficiency of Christ's work as our mediator before God, once for all.

The anchoring line runs from our souls to within the veil, where we are accepted and counted righteous by God, not because of our performance or merits, but through the work of Christ alone. The hymn writer understood this wonderful picture.

When darkness veils His lovely face,
I rest on His unchanging grace;
In every high and stormy gale,
My anchor holds within the veil.

His oath, His covenant, His blood,
Support me in the whelming flood;
When all around my soul gives way,
He then is all my hope and stay.

On Christ, the solid Rock, I stand;
All other ground is sinking sand,
All other ground is sinking sand.[10]

It is not the strength of our faith that carries us into eternity, but the sufficiency of Jesus Christ as our Prophet, Priest, Redeemer, and King. We must look to the solid Rock, Jesus Christ, trusting his righteousness alone as our standing before God. Have you put your trust in Jesus Christ alone?

We have commended our friend to the gracious provisions of Christ in the gospel, knowing that no tragic end of life can overcome the sure promises of God through Christ.

I invite you to rest your hope and confidence in Christ alone. The rest we leave with him.

Examples of Funeral Sermons

Memorial Thoughts for the Funeral of John _____ *
John 3:14 – 18

Why would a man brought up in the Mississippi Delta and a longtime resident of Memphis relocate to Spaulding, Lincolnshire, in the United Kingdom? I suppose that is a puzzling question to some of you. John _____ spent nearly half of his life educating students in the fine points of the English language. He wove together the rich history of our mother country — its Tennysons and Shakespeares and its preciseness in expressing one's deepest reflections — all in the name of teaching English and literature. He furthered this love for England by guiding tours there for many years.

Upon his retirement as a teacher in the Memphis school system, John relocated to Spaulding, a small city unknown to many of us, some sixty to seventy miles north of London. After reading a couple of John's articles in the *Lincolnshire Life* magazine, I believe I understand the wisdom of his move. He said of that area, "I felt totally at home and comfortable when I first visited Lincolnshire, loved the people, and thought the scenery was fascinating and varied. Flat land did not bother me, since I grew up in the Mississippi Delta, a vast expanse of flatness."

In this article, John admits his plan of selecting Tuesdays as his "exploration days," when, as he commented, "I paid visits to random sites, villages, and towns that somehow promised

---

* This sermon was preached at the funeral of a man living outside of the United States — someone I had never met. His sister-in-law had had numerous gospel discussions with him. His response gave us hope that he had come to faith in Christ. This sermon is an example of weaving a eulogy into a brief gospel exposition. Note that the Scripture used in this message is taken from the NASB.

fulfillment of my nebulous requirement of 'sounding interesting.'" He added, "I was never disappointed, having incredible days out, seeing a myriad of new things, and meeting a collage of people that began to form a patchwork of this unique county." Old towns like Bourne, Skegness, Mablethorpe, and Boston on England's eastern coastline became his new stomping grounds, looking for anything of interest, whether rivers, forests, flowers, old churches, Victorian homes, or Roman ruins. I think he sought to satisfy a thirst for understanding the land that inspired Tennyson and Shakespeare while feeling something of that inspiration in his own poetry and prose. Not too many Mississippi Delta boys chance to venture where he lived over the past ten years. But John found fulfillment in his decision.

However, not all of life is a rosy adventure. That came home to John at the end of last summer after leading a group that was touring England, when his energy level decreased and appetite disappeared. He was soon diagnosed with cancer—cancer that was advanced and rapidly draining his life. Not wanting to trouble his brother and sister-in-law, whom he dearly loved, though he talked with them every Sunday afternoon, he waited until after Christmas to tell them his sad news. That was just a little over two months ago. In conversations with John, they spoke with him about the most important issue of life—relationship to Jesus Christ.

Although John had been in church most of his life, even playing the organ during worship services for many years, he had turned away from Christ to follow his own desires. The propensity and desire that are in each of us to have our own way in life had trapped John. But the mercy of God knows no limits, nor does God's grace meet a barrier that he cannot conquer. In early conversations, John admitted his spiritual need for forgiveness and relationship with Christ. But admission and relationship to Christ are two different things. A change in the tone of his conversation was recognized about a month ago, as John spoke of being forgiven by Christ, of having turned from his sin, and of clinging to the promise of God in the powerful words of John 3:16. He told his sister-in-law that he would meditate for hours on that verse and the promise that it held for him. John even spoke to those assisting him during his illness about their need for Christ. We take encouragement from the knowledge that God's grace conquers even the most stubborn hearts, and that he is faithful to save all who will come to him through faith in Jesus Christ.

Let us take a few moments and reflect on John 3:16 and the verses that make up its context. *(Read John 3:14–18.)*

Jesus Christ spoke the most beloved verse in the New Testament, John 3:16, while dialoging with a very religious man, Nicodemus, a Pharisee and ruler among the Jews. Jesus identified him as "the teacher of Israel" (John 3:10) — one who above all others seemed to understand the Scriptures and communicate them. Yet Nicodemus did not grasp his own need before God. Though steeped in religious thought and actively involved in religious life, he failed to see how desperate he was before God.

Jesus grabbed Nicodemus's attention by telling him of the new birth: "Unless one is born again he cannot see the kingdom of God" (John 3:3). In short, Jesus wanted Nicodemus to understand that apart from the gracious intervention of God to give him new life, he would never be part of God's kingdom. Here was a man who appeared self-assured, confident, and knowledgeable, and yet Jesus helped him see that he was powerless to give himself new life. The new birth is a birth from above—a work of God by his Spirit to bring one from darkness into light, from spiritual death into spiritual life, from darkened understanding into transformed understanding of the truth. Grace leaps from these verses, showing God's power and kindness in conquering the stubbornness of our sin and rebellion against him.

Salvation is about the action of God on behalf of sinners to provide forgiveness and relationship to him. That's really what John 3:16 is about. God's love initiates his action—not merit on our part. "For God so loved the world, that He gave His only begotten [that is, his unique, one and only] Son." But this seems so foreign to our minds. How does the gracious gift of God, sending his Son from heaven to become one of the human race, to live a sinless life and then die in the place of sinners on the cross, how does that prepare us to die—and more so, to live each day before God in this world?

Jesus took Nicodemus back to a scene in the book of Numbers (chapter 21), where judgment had fallen upon the children of Israel as they complained against God and Moses in the wilderness. Fiery serpents came among them, biting them with the bite of judgment and death. The plague of serpents could not be stopped. The children of Israel were helpless and desperate for deliverance. *But God* intervened. He told Moses to make a serpent and put it on a staff, so that all who were bitten would live, by looking at the serpent that had been lifted up. That seemed so strange, did it not? Simply looking at a bronze serpent on a pole would give life to all who looked. To not look meant certain death. To look was life.

For many, Jesus Christ dying on a Roman cross seems to be a strange way for us to have life for eternity. Yet Jesus told Nicodemus, "As Moses lifted up the serpent in the wilderness, even so must the Son of Man be lifted up; so that whoever believes will in Him have eternal life" (John 3:14–15). In essence, he said to him, "Nicodemus, remember the story of the serpent in the wilderness. Moses lifted the bronze serpent on the pole, even as people around him were dying from the bite of the fiery serpents. Yet when they looked at that singular serpent, according to the promise of God, they lived. That was temporary, Nicodemus — giving life when death was so near. But what God has in store for you is much greater! The Son of Man will be lifted up, suspended between heaven and earth, to bear the judgment of God for you. As you look to him in faith, you will live forever."

Jesus Christ was lifted up so that all might see that the judgment of God fell upon the one innocent person who walked on this earth. The One who never deserved to die died on behalf of those deserving God's judgment and eternal death. Out of his great love, God gave his Son. The blows of divine judgment and wrath fell with awful power and anguish upon God's own Son as he hung on the cross. The weight of our transgressions fell upon him. He absorbed every blow of divine justice for rebels and sinners. We know for certain that God accepted the sacrifice of Jesus Christ on the cross, since three days later he raised Jesus from the dead!

Listen to the promise of God. "So that whoever believes will in Him have eternal life ... that whoever believes in Him shall not perish, but have eternal life ... He who believes in Him is not judged" (John 3:15, 16, 18). The "whoever" flings wide open the kingdom of God to all who would believe in Jesus Christ. What Christ did is for people of every tongue, tribe, race, and nationality. But it is only for those who realize their own desperate condition before God and believe in Jesus Christ, trusting his death as their very own judgment before God and relying on his resurrection as their own life from the dead.

John _____ pondered for hours this little verse. Our confidence is that in his desperate hour, when he realized he had nothing to commend himself to God, he looked and lived. That is the look of faith, the reliance on Jesus Christ alone as one's own Savior, Redeemer, and King. It is not looking to Jesus and our own merits or baptism or church membership. Look to Christ and live! No one can look for you. Look, look, look to Jesus Christ and live.

Examples of Funeral Sermons

There Is Rest in Jesus*
Matthew 11:28–30

Many things we cannot anticipate in life. We plan and imagine and dream, often mapping out what we consider the *ideal* in life. But each of us learns, often painfully, that life is not about walking in the *ideal*, as though scripted by a movie producer. Life is about facing the ups and downs, the sweet and bitter providences, the times of joy and the times of grief. The writer of Ecclesiastes understood this as perhaps few in human history have:

> There is an appointed time for everything. And there is a time for every event under heaven —
> A time to give birth and a time to die;
> A time to plant and a time to uproot what is planted.
> A time to kill and a time to heal;
> A time to tear down and a time to build up.
> A time to weep and a time to laugh;
> A time to mourn and a time to dance.
> A time to throw stones and a time to gather stones;
> A time to embrace and a time to shun embracing.
> A time to search and a time to give up as lost;
> A time to keep and a time to throw away.
> A time to tear apart and a time to sew together;
> A time to be silent and a time to speak.
> A time to love and a time to hate;
> A time for war and a time for peace.
>
> Ecclesiastes 3:1–8

* This funeral sermon was preached on January 8, 2012, at the memorial service for my granddaughter, Lyla Faye Newton. Note that the Scripture used in this message is taken from the NASB.

So how do we face those times when all of the ideals are thrown out the window and the dark, foreboding pain of grief overwhelms us? Jesus understood grief. We find him weeping at the tomb of his friend Lazarus (John 11:35). We also find him demonstrating remarkable compassion for those who were enduring grief and loss. And Jesus does not change. His compassion continues, meeting us today with fresh mercies to help us in our loss. I've found the Lord meeting me in the words we'll consider for a few moments.

A. Jesus is compassionate toward burdened people.

Jesus addresses "all who are weary and heavy-laden." The Contemporary English Version puts it this way: "If you are tired from carrying heavy burdens, come to me and I will give you rest." The context suggests that many of the people who listened to Jesus felt the heavy burden of trying to find peace through the works of the law. Some were weighed down with guilt, and there was no relief in sight. The terms Jesus used indicate that his hearers felt the heaviness in their chest or on their shoulders; something pressing on them so they could not walk in joy. It is to such people that Jesus Christ extends the invitation to *come to him with the promise of rest*.

B. Jesus issues three invitations for those who are burdened and weighed down.

1. "Come to Me." Not "come to religion" or "come to a warm, fuzzy feeling" or "come to a tradition." But come to the One who is the eternal God who became man. Come to the One who entered the human race through the virgin's womb and fully entered into human suffering and need. Come to the One who bore the burden of our sins on the cross and rose from the dead to declare that God had accepted the offering of his life in a bloody death so that every burden of sin and guilt that stands between us and God might be removed. Come to him who is exalted as Lord of all.

2. *"Take My yoke upon you."* A yoke was a W-shaped device that put two oxen together to pull a wagon or plow. The animals walked in tandem. Often a younger, weaker ox was teamed with an older, stronger one in order to teach it to plow and pull with vigor. In this picture, Jesus Christ, the strong One, invites us — the weak, helpless, and needy — to join his yoke. This means we submit to him and his strength; we put ourselves in absolute dependence on him. We do not go in and out of the yoke, but we stay in the yoke with Jesus. We do not march to our own drumbeat, but we walk in tandem with him.

3. *"Learn from Me."* It is in the yoke with Jesus — the yoke of dependence and trust and reliance — that we learn from him. We learn that his grace is sufficient for burdened people. We learn that his death for us was enough to satisfy God for eternity. We learn that a relationship to him is what life is truly about. We learn that even in the darkest moments of bitter providence that his love is just as strong, his compassion just as present, and his grace ever sufficient.

C. Jesus makes three promises for burdened people who come to him.

1. *"I will give you rest."* Rest is the opposite of anxiousness, fretting, worry, fear, doubt — it's a rest that brings peace in the middle of the storm, light in the midst of darkness, joy in the

crucible of sorrow. Come to Jesus Christ, relying on him and submitting to his yoke, and he promises rest.

2. *"You will find rest for your souls."* Even when we think there's nothing that can lift the weightiness of grief or heaviness of sorrow, coming to Jesus and learning from him, learning to rely on him, will bring the discovery of deep, intense, satisfying rest. In him, *you will find rest* for your souls.

3. *"For My yoke is easy and My burden is light."* Does that mean that following Jesus is easy or that trusting him in difficult times makes for a life without burden? No, but rather, Jesus tells us that when we trust him, when we learn from him, we will discover that a relationship to him *fits*. "Easy" does not mean simple, but rather "useful, comfortable"; in other words, his yoke is a good fit for burdened people. You discover as you learn from him that he pulls the load, so the burden we thought would drag us into the abyss is light.

We come to him who is "gentle and humble in heart," putting our necks in the yoke with him, humbling ourselves to trust him and his grace as sufficient. Our tendency is to handle the burdens of bitter providence in our own way and with our own strength. But our ways and our strengths fail. We must come to Jesus, take his yoke, and learn from him. In such simple trust, we discover an eternal rest that sustains us, even in the most difficult times. It is the yoke of Christ that I commend to you to find rest.

EXAMPLES OF FITTING EULOGIES

Brian Croft

THERE ARE SEVERAL CATEGORIES to think about as you develop a eulogy: Christian testimony, marriage, children, work, personality qualities, and service to others (military, neighbor, friends, humanitarian, etc.).

In North America, eulogies provide an opportunity for people to acknowledge the deceased's contributions to family, community, and, if appropriate, to church. However, great care must be taken to avoid eulogizing someone into heaven who showed no fruit of genuine conversion or becoming so man-centered that mourners are diverted from God and the gospel of grace.

A Eulogy for a Christian Family Member

Grandmother suffered and died, but not without hope. Because my grandmother had hope, we can grieve with hope as well. My grandmother was maybe the sweetest, kindest person I knew. She served her family like it was the great love of her life. She sacrificially cared for many of you as her life-long friends, but none of these things brought the hope she needed in her greatest time of need. The one hope she had came from her belief in what Jesus declared about himself in John 11:25–26.

What she believed about Jesus was confirmed time and time again on the Fridays we would spend with her, as she asked questions about the Bible study she was doing or discussed issues at her church with a gospel perspective in mind or just daily demonstrated a faith in Christ and a trust in his purposes.

Her faith and trust in Christ were powerfully affirmed even more in these final two months. I sat with her the day after she received news about the cancer, and she acknowledged how hard this would be. But she quickly went on to declare her trust in Christ to see her through it. I saw that trust in Christ so clearly as the pain in her back became excruciating—she cried to Jesus for comfort. I saw that trust in Jesus when I sat in the hospital with her on the final day she was alert enough to have a conversation and she asked me to read God's word to her. I would read passages about the hope we have in Christ for victory over sin and death. Often she would say, "Read that one again."

She believed this, and it empowered her to hold firmly to Christ to the end (Hebrews 3:14). Now she has the privilege to have fully experienced the words of Paul: "To live is Christ and to die is gain" (Philippians 1:21). She has now received and experiences the full inheritance that only the Son is worthy to possess, yet which Christ purchased for us by giving his own life. What else can we say but, "Hallelujah, what a Savior!"

Examples of Fitting Eulogies

A Eulogy for a Faithful Church Member

We have come to celebrate and remember the life of _____.
On behalf of her family, I would like to say thank you to those
of you who have loved, cared for, and supported them in this
difficult time. _____ was a wife, mother, sister, aunt, and
friend. Now that she is gone, she leaves behind a family and
friends saddened yet grateful to God for this life that impacted
them in so many ways.

I have loved many folks in our church who have since gone
to be with the Lord, but I have known few who have impacted
me as deeply and personally as _____ has during these
last six years I was privileged to serve as her pastor. Her encouragement, support, care, optimism, and unshakable faith in her
Savior challenged everyone who knew her. Several members of
the family will share in a few moments, but I wanted to mention a couple of ways she impacted our church as a member of
Auburndale Baptist Church for decades.

For years, she was the first person who greeted people at
church because she was there before anyone else, making coffee for the Sunday school class, even though she didn't even
drink coffee. This was just the kind of faithful servant she
was to our church for decades, and she impacted many people
because of it. One of the many ways she impacted me was the
way God used her to bring an encouraging word at the most
needed time. During a challenging time in our church when
most of the letters I was receiving were complaints, I regularly
received notes like this from _____:

Thank you for all you are doing and your faithfulness as
our pastor. I have prayed for decades that the Lord would

send a faithful man of God to our church, and the Lord has answered my prayers in you. Press on. Stay faithful. Our great God and Savior, Jesus Christ, is enough to give you strength through any difficulty you face.

She has always, and will always, have a special place with me and act as a model of what a faithful, persevering follower of Christ is. Now let us rejoice that she has received the crown of glory promised to all who hope in Christ and hold firmly to him to the end.

Examples of Fitting Eulogies

Nonchurch Member You Know

We have come to celebrate and remember the life of _____.
On behalf of his family, I would like to say thank you to those
who have loved, cared for, and supported them in this difficult time. _____ was a husband, father, grandfather,
coworker, neighbor, and friend. Now that he is gone, he leaves
behind a family and friends saddened yet grateful to God for
this life that impacted them in so many ways.

_____ was married to his wife for fifty years. In a world
that treats marriage as casual and trite, what a wonderful and
moving example to all of us of love, care, commitment, and sacrifice through the joys and struggles of marriage until the end. It
is rare to find two people who stay together for almost fifty years,
but it's just as rare, if not more so, to find a husband who con-
tinued to adore his wife the way this man did. May you not only
be challenged to be committed through the joys and struggles
in your own marriage in the same way these two modeled—but
husbands, may you love, serve, and adore your wife the same way
this man clearly and consistently did for fifty years.

It also sounds like words do not do justice to describe how
much this man loved his family. It has been said that you know
the character of a person by the way his children speak about
him. What a powerful testimony to hear this man's children
say so many endearing things about him—things like,

- We always knew he loved us.
- He would have given us anything if he could.
- He guided us through life like no one else.
- He was always at every activity to support us, even if he
  didn't like the activity.

- He called us every day.
- He was easy to talk to.
- He was very wise.
- He always kissed us good night.
- He always walked us to the door when we left.
- He was always there for us.

If you get the impression he deeply loved his children and that they were his life—well, I'm told you have to multiply this love several times for his ten grandchildren! So many people in this world cannot even say they have a good relationship with their father or grandfather, yet the children and grandchildren of this man couldn't have imagined a better one. That is definitely something to remember and celebrate.

_____ was also a very hard and faithful worker, evidenced most clearly in his highly decorated military career. Half of this lengthy obituary you picked up on your way in is devoted to listing the awards and honors he was given in twenty-eight years of serving our country. We should feel safe and confident if those who currently serve our country possess half the bravery, courage, and commitment to their country as this man had during his lifetime.

One of my first encounters and most memorable moments of this man and of his family took place at his daughter's wedding reception as the wedding party was being introduced. All of a sudden, just as though an announcer straight out of professional wrestling had taken the stage, "the General and Big Doll" were introduced, the crowd went wild. I was standing there waiting for two costumed mascots to walk through the door when instead it was the bride's parents! I can remember thinking, "This has to be an interesting man who leads this family."

After spending some time with him over these past ten years at different family gatherings, several things struck me, but one in particular stands out—something that is very rare in this world. This man was a decorated Vietnam war hero—a man's man with strong opinions—and yet every encounter I had with him showed a man who was gentle, kind, warm, and thoughtful. He was a man who seemed to desire to serve others more than himself. And certainly so much of what the family told me about him just confirmed these unique qualities as having been consistently true throughout his life. It is good for us to take the time to remember these wonderful character qualities and celebrate his life today.

Nonchurch Member You Do Not Know

We have come to celebrate and remember the life of _____.
Whether it was her forty-year marriage to her husband, her tender moments of care and instruction with her children, her charitable efforts to serve the less fortunate, or her hobbies that all who knew her benefited from, this woman's life impacted family, friends, coworkers, and neighbors alike.

Her family dearly loved her and was most impacted by her, particularly her sister and all the time they were able to spend together. Also, her grandchildren had a special love for her. There seemed to be a theme in her life of not only her love for her family, but also their deep love and appreciation for her. May you be challenged, by the way she loved and cared for her children and grandchildren, to go and do likewise.

I'm told she was a tenacious worker, as this defined so much of who she was. In a world where many are lazy, unmotivated, and unwilling to be faithful to their responsibilities, what an amazing example we had in this woman who not only worked hard to care for her home and family but labored hard outside her home to provide for those she cared for. May you be challenged by her incredible work ethic and be motivated to make the most of your time and efforts, as she clearly did.

She had a deep love for other people. I'm told that no matter whether it was her family, coworkers, or friends, she would do anything she could to help someone in need. She seemed to be more concerned about others and their well-being than about herself. What a tremendous example of compassion, love, humility, and empathy to those hurting and in need. All of us would be better off by following her example of faithfulness.

Examples of Fitting Eulogies

Unknown Adult with Mental Disabilities

We have come to celebrate and remember the life of _____.
We all are impacted by different kinds of people in our lives
and for different reasons. However, there are those rare occasions when we are given the gift of knowing someone who
impacts us in special ways that the most talented and charis-
matic cannot — someone who makes us better and causes us
to view the world differently than we would have otherwise.
_____ was this type of special, unique individual whose
qualities affected everyone who knew her.

The most shining of her qualities that seemed to impact
others was her great love for her family and friends. As I looked
through the pictures of her life, it is obvious that not only did
she love her family; they loved her deeply as well. Her family could always be confident they would experience a pleas-
ant smile, a kind word, and a warm embrace from her. Many
people in this world are never loved like this, but _____'s
family was blessed to have this experience every time they were
with her. I think it is safe to say that people like _____
not only love us in a special way but teach us how to love others by the way they love. May you be challenged to love others
with the same commitment, depth, and zeal that this woman
modeled for each of us.

I'm told _____ was a hard worker and was faithful
and dependable. This was seen in the fact that not only did she
regularly show up at work, but she even went to work when she
wasn't sure there would be much work to do. In a world where
many people are lazy and negligent of their responsibilities,
even though they have nothing to hinder them from working

hard, what an amazing example this woman was to so many of us. Now may we be challenged to emulate her example of this same kind of work ethic.

She had an amazing perspective on life that allowed her to smile, have joy, and be content, regardless of the difficulties that came her way. This is a powerful testimony in itself, but when we add the challenges that came with her disabilities, it strengthens this testimony even more. Several years ago, a friend's daughter was born with the same disability that _____ had. When my friend called his pastor to tell him the news, the pastor wisely replied, "It sounds like two special parents were given a special little girl." This seems to profoundly capture God's perspective.

The world wants to refer to these qualities as disabilities or hindrances to living life, but this is not the perspective of the God who created all things and makes no mistakes. _____'s family and friends, who spoke of her with such love—who spoke as people who learned how to have a greater love for others, appreciation for their work, and a joyful perspective on life—would disagree with the world's perspective also. Now that she is gone, you will honor this woman and her life by living your life with the same unique and special perspective that she did, and in doing so, you will celebrate and remember her life.

Examples of Fitting Eulogies

Unknown Adult (Known to Have Hurt Others)

We have come to remember the life of _____. On behalf of his family I would like to say thank you to those of you who have loved, cared for, and supported them in this difficult time. _____ was a husband, father, grandfather, brother, coworker, neighbor, and friend. Now that he is gone, he leaves behind a family and friends saddened as they reflect back and remember his life.

Some of you are saddened because of the things about his life that you will miss—things you want to celebrate. The twenty-five years of marriage he celebrated with his wife, his outgoing personality to which many were drawn, his jokes and the times of laughter and cutting up together, his military service, the way he interacted with the nursing home workers and had a close relationship with them, the memories of those who were with him in his final days to see the remorse of past mistakes and the weighty accountability that comes to those who are moments from meeting their Creator. Some of you are saddened because these memories mean that he is gone, and you will miss these things about his life that were good.

Yet some of you are saddened as we remember this man's life because of your relationship with him—a relationship that wasn't what you had hoped it would be. Instead of grieving the loss of someone, you find yourself dealing with regret, trying to forgive and move forward in your life now that he is gone. Though painful, this is also a part of the grieving process, and it's a good thing to embrace and walk through as we take some time this morning to reflect and remember this man's life.

EXAMPLES OF APPROPRIATE MUSIC

Phil Newton with Jim Carnes

"A Debtor to Mercy Alone" (Augustus Montague Toplady)

"A Mighty Fortress Is Our God" (Martin Luther)

"Abide with Me" (Henry Francis Lyte)

"All I Have Is Christ" (Jordan Kauflin)

"Alleluia! Sing to Jesus!" (William Chatterton Dix)

"Amazing Grace" (John Newton)

"Be Still, My Soul" (Katharina A. von Schlegel)

"Be Thou My Vision" (Ancient Irish Hymn)

"Before the Throne of God Above" (Charitie Lees Bancroft)

"Children of the Heavenly Father" (Karolina Wilhelmina
    Sandell-Berg)

"Christ Jesus Lay in Death's Strong Bands" (Martin Luther)

"Christ the Lord Is Risen Again" (Michael Weisse; trans.
    Catherine Winkworth)

"Fairest Lord Jesus" (Münster Gesangbuch; trans. Joseph
    August Seiss)

"For All the Saints" (William Walsham How)

"Glory Is Certain" (Henry Francis Lyte and David Ward)

"Guide Me, O Thou Great Jehovah" (William Williams)

"Holy, Holy, Holy! Lord God Almighty" (Reginald Heber)

"How Firm a Foundation" ("K" in John Rippon's *Selection of Hymns*)

"How Great Thou Art" (Stuart K. Hine)

"How Sweet and Aweful Is the Place" (Isaac Watts)

"How Sweet the Name of Jesus Sounds" (John Newton)

"I Need Thee Every Hour" (Annie S. Hawks)

"I Will Glory in My Redeemer" (Steve and Vikki Cook)

"If Thou But Suffer God to Guide Thee" (Georg Neumark; trans. Catherine Winkworth)

"Immortal, Invisible, God Only Wise" (Walter Chalmers Smith)

"In Christ Alone" (Keith and Kristyn Getty)

"It Is Well with My Soul" (Horatio G. Spafford)

"Lift High the Cross" (George William Kitchin and Michael Robert Newbolt)

"Like a River Glorious" (Frances Ridley Havergal)

"Lord Jesus, Think on Me" (Synesius of Cyrene)

"Love Divine, All Loves Excelling" (Charles Wesley)

"My Faith Looks Up to Thee" (Ray Palmer)

"Not What My Hands Have Done" (Horatius Bonar)

"Now Thank We All Our God" (Martin Rinkart; trans. Catherine Winkworth)

"O for a Thousand Tongues to Sing" (Charles Wesley)

"O God, Our Help in Ages Past" (Isaac Watts)

"O Worship the King, All Glorious Above" (Robert Grant)

"Praise, My Soul, the King of Heaven" (Henry Francis Lyte)

"Praise to the Lord, the Almighty" (Joachim Neander; trans. Catherine Winkworth)

"Rock of Ages" (Augustus Montague Toplady)

Examples of Appropriate Music

"The King of Love My Shepherd Is" (Henry W. Baker)

"The Lord Is My Shepherd" (James Montgomery)

"The Old Rugged Cross" (George Bennard)

"The Sands of Time Are Sinking" (Anne Ross Cousin based on the letters of Samuel Rutherford)

"The Solid Rock" (Edward Mote)

"The Strife Is O'er, the Battle Done" (*Symphonia Sirenum Selectarum*; trans. Francis Pott)

"What a Friend We Have in Jesus" (Joseph Scriven)

"Whate'er My God Ordains Is Right" (Samuel Rodigast; trans. Catherine Winkworth)

"What Wondrous Love Is This" (American Folk Hymn)

EXAMPLES OF ORDER OF FUNERAL SERVICES

Brian Croft

Example #1

Scripture Reading Psalm 145:17 – 21
Song "Praise to the Lord, the Almighty"
Welcome
Eulogy
Prayer Prayer for family
Song "Abide with Me"
Sermon John 11
Prayer Prayer of hope in Christ
Song "Amazing Grace"
Closing Scripture Reading 1 Corinthians 15:50 – 58

Example #2

Scripture Reading Psalm 99
Song "Holy, Holy, Holy, Lord God Almighty"
Welcome
Prayer Prayer of hope in Christ
Scripture Reading Romans 5:1 – 11
Song "The Solid Rock"
Testimony Family member or friend

Eulogy
Prayer Prayer of comfort for family
Song "I Need Thee Every Hour"
Scripture Reading 1 Thessalonians 4:13 – 18
Prayer Prayer of hope of resurrection
Sermon John 14:1 – 6
Closing Prayer

Example #3
Song "Amazing Grace"
Scripture Reading Ephesians 2:1 – 10
Welcome
Prayer Prayer of hope in Christ
Song "O for a Thousand Tongues to Sing"
Testimony Family member
Eulogy
Prayer Prayer of comfort for family
Scripture Reading Psalm 23
Song "It Is Well with My Soul"
Sermon Hebrews 12:1 – 3
Closing Prayer

Example of Graveside Service Only
Scripture Psalm 46
Welcome
Prayer Prayer for family
Brief Eulogy
Short Homily John 11
Prayer Prayer of hope in Christ

NOTES

1. John Flavel, Sermon 37 in "The Fountain of Life," in *The Works of John Flavel* (Carlisle, PA: Banner of Truth, 1997), 1:466.

2. Richard Baxter, *The Practical Works of the Rev. Richard Baxter* (London: Paternoster, 1830), 1:121.

3. Charles Haddon Spurgeon, *Lectures to My Students* (1881; repr., Pasadena, TX: Pilgrim, 1990), 2:179.

4. Theocritus, quoted in F. F. Bruce, *1 and 2 Thessalonians,* Word Bible Commentary (Nashville: Nelson, 1982), 96.

5. Augustine, quoted in Peter Gorday, ed., *Colossians, 1 – 2 Thessalonians, 1 – 2 Timothy, Titus, Philemon,* Ancient Christian Commentary on Scripture (Downers Grove, IL: InterVarsity, 2000), 85.

6. See, for example, John Piper, *The Swans Are Not Silent,* 5 vols. (Wheaton, IL: Crossway); J. I. Packer, *A Grief Sanctified* (Wheaton, IL: Crossway, 2002); James W. Bruce III, *From Grief to Glory* (Carlisle, PA: Banner of Truth, 2008); Elisabeth Elliot, *Facing the Death of Someone You Love* (Wheaton, IL: Crossway, 1980); John Murray, *Behind a Frowning Providence* (Carlisle, PA: Banner of Truth, 1990).

7. See Gaius Davies, *Genius, Grief and Grace: A Doctor Looks at Suffering and Success* (Fearn, Ross-shire,

Scotland: Christian Focus, 2001), for a number of helpful studies, including one on William Cowper (pp. 93 – 122).

8. Paul Tautges (*Comfort Those Who Grieve* [Leominster, UK: Day One, 2009], 104 – 6) has an excellent chart that I commend to you for further help with postfuneral pastoral care.

9. Quoted in R. Albert Mohler Jr. and Daniel Akin, "The Salvation of the 'Little Ones': Do Infants Who Die Go to Heaven?" July 16, 2009, www.albertmohler .com/2009/07/16/the-salvation-of-the-little-ones-do -infants-who-die-go-to-heaven/ (accessed October 11, 2013).

10. Edward Mote, "The Solid Rock," stanzas 2 and 3.

Practical
Shepherding

The Practical Shepherding series provides pastors and ministry leaders with practical help to do the work of pastoral ministry in a local church. The seven-volume series, when complete, will include:

- *Conduct Gospel-Centered Funerals: Applying the Gospel at the Unique Challenges of Death*
- *Prepare Them to Shepherd: Test, Train, Affirm, and Send the Next Generation of Leaders*
- *Visit the Sick: Ministering God's Grace in Times of Illness*
- *Comfort the Grieving: Ministering God's Grace in Times of Loss* (Available February 2015)
- *Understand, Plan, and Lead Worship: Applying Biblical Doctrine and Spirituality to Christian Worship* (Available February 2015)
- *Pray for the Flock: Ministering God's Grace through Intercession* (Available August 2015)
- *Exercise Oversight: Shepherding the Flock through Administration and Delegation* (Available August 2015)

In addition to the series, be sure to look for these titles by Brian and Cara Croft on the pastor's family and ministry:

- *The Pastor's Family* by Brian and Cara Croft
- *The Pastor's Ministry* by Brian Croft (Available April 2015)